Dharma Girl

Acknowledgments

First thanks to you, Dad—for once telling me that a girl without freckles is like a night without stars, and for saying the right thing ever since. I also owe a huge debt to a few special people without whose help this book wouldn't exist, namely Holly Morris, my talented editor at Seal, who has the eerie ability of knowing what I'm trying to say better than I do, Tom Simmons at the University of Iowa, who convinced me this was a book and made its publication possible and Janet Silver at Houghton Mifflin whose kindness and encouragement I will always be grateful for. Thanks also to my agent, Christina Ward (the fax machine works now, really), Professor Judy Polumbaum, Professor Paul Von Blum and my high school English teacher, Mrs. Doud—who told me that I was a writer and that there was no getting out of it. Thank you Laura, for reminding me to walk with my bare feet on, Tom, for the Shetland ponies, Cecily, Pat, Ken, Jeremy, Donnie, Frank, and everyone else whose high hearts welcomed me back to Iowa City, and of course, my love to Shelley, Curt, Cunningham, Colleen, Elliott, Krista, Randy, Richard, and all the rest who helped me look for berries.

Seal Press
3131 Western Avenue, Suite 410
Seattle, Washington 98121
Email: sealprss@scn.org

Cover design by Kate Thompson
Cover photograph courtesy of K. Knudsen/WestStock.
Copyright © 1992.
Text design by Stacy M. Lewis

Printed in the United States of America
First printing, November 1996
1 2 3 4 5 6 7 8 9 10

Library of Congress Cataloging-in-Publication Data
Cain, Chelsea.
Dharma girl: a road trip across the American generations /
Chelsea Cain.
1. Cain, Chelsea. 2. Young women—United States—Biography.
3. Hippies—United States—Biography. 4. Communal living—
Iowa—Iowa City. I. Title.
CT275.C18A3   1996   973.92'092—dc20   96-23697
ISBN 1-878067-89-3
ISBN 1-878067-84-2 (pbk)

Distributed to the trade by Publishers Group West
In Canada: Publishers Group West Canada, Toronto, Canada
In Europe and the U.K.: Airlift Book Company, London, England

Dharma Girl

A Road Trip Across
the American Generations

Chelsea Cain

SEAL PRESS

SEATTLE

For my mother, the Snowqueen.

And the skin is thin,
The great big round seed
In the middle,
Is your own Original Nature—
Pure and smooth,
Almost nobody ever splits it open
Or ever tries to see
If it will grow.

— from "Avocado," by Gary Snyder

Prologue

June 1995. I have been walking a lot lately. It is an odd compulsion. I leave my apartment. I start walking. I have no idea where I'm going. Sometimes, after ten or twelve blocks, I will look up and know exactly where I am. I will be standing in front of one of the old houses I used to live in or the hospital where I was born or the park where my dad tried to teach me how to throw a frisbee. And sometimes, I will walk and walk, and not recognize anything at all.

My mother, before she leaves, says that I walk as an excuse for thinking. She says that it is easier to walk through thoughts than to sit in a dark room and mull over them. But I am a Californian, I tell her; when I need to think, I drive. She laughs, and her voice sounds hollow over the phone line. The

3

next day she heads for Mexico. Three months, she says, but I don't think she's coming back.

It is spring, which isn't saying much in Iowa. Tornado season. I walk until the rain starts and keep my eye out for twisters. Yesterday morning it was sunny and I sat by the Iowa River and tried to remember my parents. Not the people I know now, but who they were then, back when they were twenty and still believed that Richard Nixon couldn't be elected president. This was before Kent State and Cambodia, before my dad was drafted, before they made the decisions that would eventually deliver us all to a commune just outside of Iowa City. Before I would leave Iowa with my mother as a six-year-old to grow up on the West Coast. Before I would come back to Iowa seventeen years later.

Today there is a severe weather watch. I carry my red umbrella like a light saber, tapping it on the ground every so often to mark my steps. I am suspended in my past here, and in the past of my parents. I sit in crowded restaurants and I look around at people my parents' age, and I wonder—did they know them? I want to understand who they were, those two longhaired, young people smiling up at me from already aging photographs. I want to understand who we all were. Who we are.

It is, I think, the reason why I walk.

My parents still cannot talk about the war in Vietnam without bitterness. Fifty-eight thousand dead. Fifty-eight thousand of a generation dead in a war that should never have been fought. "You can't know what that's like," my father says. Fifty-eight thousand.

I grew up knowing the weight of this number. I was born three years before Saigon fell, on a hippie commune in the middle of America, and I am still somehow a child of that war. I am reminded of this by the relics of my youth. The poster in my kindergarten classroom that read "War is not healthy for children and other living things." The music. How my parents chose to raise me. These fragments of my past are still with me. They create the veil through which I see life;

4

they are the basis of all my assumptions about government and patriotism and politics. They smile at me from behind the eyes of those old photographs, they hum along to the lyrics of Bob Dylan, they sit deep in my chest when I read about Robert McNamara.

I carry them with me everywhere.

The child who I was is five years old. She has bright blonde hair that is uncombed, and wears a dirty red velvet dress. She does not wear shoes and she carries a big plastic doll even though the doll disappeared, along with the dress, almost eighteen years ago.

The girl I became grew up far from Iowa City. She is the daughter of hippies, unsure of how to fit into the world. She changes her middle name because Elizabeth sounds better than Snow. She stops calling her parents by their first names and starts calling them Mom and Dad. She does not tell her friends about the commune or her father's draft resistance or her old goat, Full Moon.

The young woman I am has come back to Iowa because she still has something she needs to understand. She has her father's narrow blue eyes and her mother's grin. She speaks with her mother's light voice, and has her habit of inappropriate laughter. Her father's gestures grow out of her hands, and his politics are heavy in her stomach. She is both their daughters. She walks with both their steps—her father's long strides, her mother's arm swing. She reads their books. She listens to their music. She is trying to understand her parents through their generation and their generation through her generation and her generation through her own true self and her own true self through her parents, and, as you can imagine, this has made her very tired.

So she has gone off on a walk, which is when I catch up with her.

"I know exactly what you're going through," I say, accidentally smacking her in the back of the knee with my umbrella. She is tall and thin, about a year younger than I am.

She looks at me and sighs. "I wish you'd leave me alone," she says, speeding up.

I match my gait to hers, so that we are walking side by side, each swinging the outside arm. We look like a child's bathtub toy paddling through soapy water. "Look. You have everything you need. You have your parents' stories. You've traveled all the way back to Iowa. All you have to do is make sense of it, right?"

"It's not that easy," she says, flustered. "I am a very complex person, and besides, all this generational deconstruction involves a lot of sociopolitical theory that I haven't finished researching yet." I can tell she doesn't think she's ready for this yet, and I remind myself that she has just been here a couple of days and that it has only been a month since she knew for certain that she had to go back to Iowa. She is still that same person, the one who suddenly, improbably, decided one day that the life she was living was not the one those hippies on that farm had wanted for her. But this her, the one she still is, doesn't know if there is any way to get that back.

I reach into my heavy book bag and pull out a two-hundred-page bound manuscript. She cringes and backs away. "Just look at it," I say, trying to force the manuscript into her hands. "It's about my trip back to Iowa and the hippie commune my parents lived on. Read the first few chapters. I really think you'll find it helpful."

"Look," she says. "I said no and I meant no. I don't have that kind of time." She is wearing sweatpants, a University of California at Irvine sweatshirt, a headband and white sneakers with purple swooshes on the sides. It is a look that took her four years to cultivate, although it is exactly the same as everyone else's she went to school with, which was, of course, the point.

"Please. I think you really need to read this."

She stops walking and puts her hands on her hips like her father. "Oh, all right," she says, taking the manuscript from me with a toss of her blonde hair. "Fine. Fine. Okay, I'll read it. Are you happy?"

I nod. She sighs once more, snorts loudly and then walks quickly off, turning back every so often to make sure I'm not following her.

I watch her go.

She doesn't know it yet, but she is about to run into herself. She is a psychonaut—a voyager into the soul—and since she has read the *Tibetan Book of the Dead* she will soon realize that in order to find herself, she first has to create a self to identify. She has to tell the story. She has to find the child she was and the girl she became to get the answers she wants. She has to see if she can find what she has lost track of, before she can go on to anything else.

*The best thing, of course, is not
to get lost. One way to avoid it
is first to get acquainted with the
country where you camp. Make
yourself a small pocket map
showing the essential landmarks
around camp so that you can
always find your way back.*
—The Handbook For Boys,
Boy Scouts of America

June 1994. I am driving from Oregon to Iowa
in my old tan Honda Accord to look for Snowbird. It is summertime and it is hot and humid
and the air conditioner is loud and cold. I have

brought with me my books and albums and clothes, a tin of Altoids Peppermints, a bag of grapefruit, a blank journal and my mother, who has eaten four of the mints and most of the grapefruit.

We are trying to get to Pocatello by nightfall and conversation has become grim, so we spend the next few hours riding in silence, watching the bugs smack against the windshield.

After a while, my mother comes up with a game to pass the time where we try to see how many phrases we can come up with that somehow incorporate the open road. She writes them in the journal.

"Hit the road, Jack."

"Road weary."

"Road wise."

"Road warrior."

"Highway to heaven."

"I'll take the high way, you take the low way."

"High road to China."

She puts down the pen. "When we get to Iowa," she says, "I want to have my picture taken standing in a corn field in my bra and panties."

We pull over at a rest stop and get out to stretch our legs, and my mother goes inside to pee. There is a busload of Christian choir singers ahead of us so she has to wait in line, and I sit on the curb enjoying the feel of the warm cement beneath my bare feet.

She comes out after about ten minutes and we get back into the car, only this time it is my turn to ride in the passenger's seat. My stereo is wrapped in a comforter on the floor so I stretch my legs up onto the dashboard, noticing my smudgy toe prints on the windshield.

"Don't put your feet up there," my mother says.

I pretend to be asleep.

~

I have a favorite photograph of my mother. She is sitting on a grassy hill, her arm around a young man, and they are smiling. She has long, straight brown hair and she is wearing a red minidress that shows off her long, pale legs. She is barefoot, young and beautiful.

The photograph was taken in 1970 in front of my parents' first apartment in Davenport, Iowa, a few weeks before my dad was drafted. The apartment was on Oneida Street, which my mother would later jokingly recall had also been the name of the most successful of a collection of religious communes that sprouted in the Midwest in the mid-nineteenth century.

In another photograph of my mother, she is standing in front of her parents' house holding up a sign that says East Coast in big, black, handwritten letters. She is wearing a faded red kerchief in her hair and carrying a big backpack she used to take with her hitchhiking. My father isn't in the picture because he is explaining to his parents why he has to leave the country.

"I know you're not asleep," my mother says, and I groan and take my feet off the dashboard. I open my eyes just in time to see a highway sign fly past. *Bliss 7 miles.*

I turn my head toward my mother. "We're going back to Iowa," I say.

"Yes," she says. "I know."

S nowbird wakes up every morning to the sun spilling through yellow curtains, but this morning is different.

She wakes up restless. The house is too quiet.

She sits up and puts her small, bare feet on the wood floor. Her bedroom is on the first floor in this house, so she has to pad through the living room past the woodstove which is still glowing dark-orange light, and the couch where someone is sleeping, his face so buried in the seat cushion that she wonders if he is breathing.

She climbs the cold, wooden steps past the landing to the second floor and down the long hall to the room where her parents sleep.

It is cold upstairs.

She opens the door and sees them both asleep

in bed. Her father sees her, stirs himself awake and comes to the doorway. He is naked.

"It's morning," she says. Time to get up.

"No," he tells her. "It's the middle of the night."

Snowbird shakes her head. No. It's light.

He stands there for a minute looking at her as she stares up at him. He breathes, blinks a couple of times. Then he takes her by the hand and leads her to the window at the end of the hall. There are no curtains or blinds and she sees that it is deep, black night.

"It's cold," he says. "I'm going back to bed."

But she shakes her head again and pulls his large fingers until he follows her downstairs, past the woodstove and the sleeping man who hasn't moved and into her bedroom where the yellow light is still glowing in the window over her bed.

"Oh," he says, looking at the light and understanding. "It's the porch light. Someone has left the porch light on."

He sits her on the bed and disappears into the living room. In an instant the yellow light is gone. Day is night again. Light is dark. And she sits there on the bed, looking out the window into the black, sensing that she has just learned something very important but not knowing what yet, until her father comes back in moving quickly to keep warm and tucks her under her red and green quilt.

"See?" he says.

And she nods.

When she gets a little older, Snowbird spends most of her time looking for berries. This involves much effort plodding through the gardens lifting each individual leaf to see if a strawberry is hiding beneath it. (She is supposed to save the berries in a pail, but in the excitement she usually ends up eating them.)

Snowbird likes to hunt for berries for three reasons: she likes the way they taste (except the green ones), she likes the search and she likes the freedom of wandering around the farm in her blue terry cloth underpants because, for the most part, she is completely on her own.

This freedom is not without qualifications, however, and there are two rules that she must always know: NEVER LET THE DOGS INTO THE SHEEP PEN and DON'T GO INTO THE CHICKEN COOP WITHOUT SHOES ON.

On this day, she and her father forget the second rule and when she goes with him to check for eggs, she steps on a big piece of brown glass.

Her dad carries her back to the house and then he and her mother and she all drive to University Hospital in Iowa City where she gets seven stitches on the bottom of her foot.

"DON'T GO INTO THE CHICKEN COOP WITHOUT SHOES ON," her mother says again.

Her father looks away.

While her foot is healing, Snowbird spends her days sitting on the porch in the sun with the dogs. Since she is the only child on the farm she spends a lot of time entertaining herself. She makes up songs to sing to the dogs or she plays with her toy cars (her favorite is the purple Volkswagen beetle) or she feeds the dogs their food piece by piece and eats a few pieces herself.

There is always music at the farm. Van Morrison. The Grateful Dead. The Beatles. Bob Dylan. Bonnie Raitt. Joni Mitchell. She knows all the words to all the songs and sometimes her dad and some of the others will play guitars and banjos on the porch at night, and she gets to sing.

There are big dinners in the evenings. Lots of people, some who live at the farm and some who don't, sit around the big table in the kitchen or on the porch in the summer, drinking beer and smoking and talking about the war and why Richard Nixon shouldn't be president.

Her dad didn't fight in the war. He got his draft notice and decided not to go. She knew this early on because there was a green scrub suit he put on sometimes to go to work at the hospital where he was serving his alternative duty sentence. Her parents explained to her that they had lived underground for two years before her father turned himself into the FBI. She had been at the sentencing, but she was too young to remember. "Wear a dress and bring the baby," her father's lawyer had told her mother. He later quit the law to go write novels on the Left Bank.

There is always music at the farm, but today it is quiet because her mother and Colleen are harvesting vegetables from the garden, Bob and Fern are in South America, Curt and Shelley are upstairs, her father and Elliott and Cunningham and Donnie have all gone into town to buy fifty-pound bags of dog food and shoplift cold cases of Pabst Blue Ribbon, and Marta, who is visiting from Europe, is reading *War and Peace*.

It is quiet, so Snowbird enjoys the hot sun on her face and the sound her cars make on the wooden porch. Her foot does not hurt so much anymore, but now her stomach is sore from eating too many dried pellets of dog food.

"What are you doing?" Marta asks, looking up from her book. She is sitting on the worn mauve couch on the porch, her bare, tan legs stretched forward and crossed at the ankles. "Are you playing Indy 500?"

"No," Snowbird says. She isn't driving the car. She *is* the car. She is the purple Volkswagen beetle and she can feel her tires vibrate on the wood and the heat on her hood and the breeze that blows on her windshield when she pushes really fast. *She is the car.*

She looks up at Marta, but Marta is determined to finish *War and Peace* before she goes back to Europe, and has already gone back to reading.

W here did the name Snowbird come from?" I ask my mother. She is still driving, but in the last hour her long body has reclined so far into the seat that I am beginning to wonder if she can see out the windshield.

"I think it was because you were born during that blizzard of 1972," she says.

"No," I groan. (She never remembers this kind of thing.) "That's why you gave me the name Snow. But why did you all call me Snowbird?"

She squints her eyes and raises one eyebrow a little, thinking.

"Okay. Who called me Snowbird first? Was it my dad? Was it Donnie?" Donnie had been my favorite person at the farm. The nephew of the old woman who owned it, he stopped by to "check up on the hippies," and ended up moving in.

"Oh," she says, "I don't know. It was so long ago. I forget sometimes that you went by that at all. Anyway, I wanted to call you Sky Blue."

I let that last part go. "Who do you think would remember?"

She squints again. Raises an eyebrow. "Your dad, probably. I think he called you that the most. But he hasn't called you Snowbird in years, has he?"

"No," I say. "Not since Iowa."

"You're going where?" my roommate, Molly, asked me when I told her I was leaving California.

"Iowa," I repeated. "It's part of that big space you have to fly over to get to New York City."

"I know where Iowa is," she lied. "What about California? You love it here."

"I don't want to live in California anymore," I told her. "The whole time I've lived here I've gone by Chelsea Elizabeth Cain. That's not even my real name. My real name is Chelsea Snow. I don't even like the name Chelsea Elizabeth— it sounds like a cosmetics company."

Molly looked at me from under her perfectly even bangs. "What are you talking about?"

"Elizabeth isn't my real name. It's one I made up in sixth grade when a cute boy asked me my middle name and I was too embarrassed to say Snow because then he would know that my parents had been whacked-out, hippie potheads."

"But everyone thinks your name is Chelsea Elizabeth. I mean, it's on your driver's license."

"Well," I said, "It sort of stuck."

"You made it up? Just like that?"

"Yeah."

"And now you want to go back to Iowa so you can be Chelsea Snow again?"

"Uh huh."

"And Iowa is where you lived on that farm with your parents and a bunch of hippies and dogs, right?"

"Yeah. I'm going to drive up to Portland and pick up my mom and we're going to make a road trip out of it."

Molly looked at me, concentrating. "Let me get this straight. You're going to move to Iowa because you want to change your middle name?"

"Yes."

"Why?"

"I'm looking for *dharma*." (I didn't know exactly what it meant, but I liked the sound of it.)

She looked pained. *"Dharma."*

"You know. It's like the path to knowledge or something. It's Buddhist."

"You've been watching those Bill Moyers specials again, haven't you?"

"No."

"Yes you have. Remember after they reran that mind-body special and you tried to convince all my sorority sisters that you could read their thoughts?"

"That was different."

"Uh huh."

"Besides, I've been meaning to move back to Iowa for years. It just took me a little while to figure it out."

Molly sighed. Underneath her chair I could hear one of her Doc Martens tapping lightly against the carpet. Across the table she eyed me suspiciously—it was the same look she used to give the new Becky after the old Becky was replaced on "Roseanne."

But my mind was already twirling east. Toward Iowa. Toward Snowbird. Toward the farm, rusty windmills, the Grateful Dead and lightning bugs. We weren't just returning. We were voyaging, passaging and pilgrimaging. I was bound to find *something*.

≈

19

The Snowqueen is Snowbird's spirit guide. Sometimes when Snowbird least expects it the Snowqueen will come down from the moon and leave Snowbird gifts and handwritten notes like this one:

"To my small friend, Snowbird—You have never met me but I know exactly who you are. Tomorrow is a very special day for me. It is called the winter solstice. Some people call it the first day of winter. Will you celebrate this day with me? Here are some gifts for you, my new friend. Sometimes when you are either very happy or else very sad and feel too much alone, look at the moon very hard. Then squint your eyes and I think you will see me. I love you. — The Snowqueen."

One day, when Snowbird is in her little room playing with the plastic horses from her mother, the doorbell rings. Snowbird waits for her mother to answer it, but when the bell rings again, she leaves the horses on the floor and goes to the door. There is no one there and she is just about to go back to her toys when she sees the white pillowcase on the porch.

She drags the bag into the kitchen and calls for her mother.

"It's presents from the Snowqueen," Snowbird cries. She opens the pillowcase and pulls out two new books and a red plastic viewfinder.

Her mother appears from the living room. "The Snowqueen knew how much you wanted that viewfinder," she says.

Snowbird smiles and nods, still unsure of why she is so lucky and why the Snowqueen is so kind. She slips a cartridge into the viewfinder and snaps the advance lever. The cartoon inside clicks forward.

Her mother squats down on the linoleum beside her. "The Snowqueen is your very own guardian angel," she explains. "She is your *bodhisattva*. Do you know what that means?"

Snowbird shakes her head.

"It means she is someone who will help you on your *dharma* path. She will guide you."

"Like Mother Bear?"

"She is kind like Mother Bear, and wise like Miss Clavel. She is tall like the man in the big yellow hat, and clever like Sal and Madeleine."

Snowbird looks up from the viewfinder. "Can she see me right now?"

"Always," her mother says. "And when you need her, she will be right there to help you find whatever you are looking for."

The first animal we see on our trip is a coyote. We're still in Idaho, heading for Pocatello, past the burning range fires and the third of a hundred trains we will see on this trip. Past the trailer parks and the black-and-white dairy cows. Past the highway signs that say *Historical Sight* with arrows pointing at seemingly empty fields.

My mother sees it first.

"Look," she whispers.

The coyote is absolutely motionless. Rigid. It stands on the side of the freeway, its legs shoulder-width apart, perfectly planted on the road. A mangy thing, up close—its gold coat is the color of the dried fields the farmers have been burning. My mother slows down as we pass it and all of a sudden there are no cars ahead of or behind us. The whole world is just this coyote, my mother and me. I watch it watching us, the head turning only to follow us as we pass.

A few miles up we see another coyote, dead at the side of the road.

"That must be her mate," my mother says. "She's trying to find him."

We will see her again and again, after that—through Idaho, Wyoming, Nebraska—always at the side of the road, always looking.

"Amazing, isn't it?" my mother asks.

"What?"

"That there are any coyotes left who *haven't* been killed by cars."

My mother was dying. But not yet.

Looking back now, my journey back to Iowa began with that one cancer cell that grew and multiplied in a mole on the back of her left shoulder. This was in 1992. Spring. She went to a clinic to have the mole looked at when it started changing shape and they immediately did a biopsy. When she returned for the results one of the doctors passed her in the hall and said, "I'm so sorry." That's how she found out she had melanoma.

At the time, I was still in college in California, living in Irvine, a stucco city where it is illegal to paint your house an unsanctioned color and you can be fined for leaving your garage door open too long because it is considered unsightly. I could not, in other words, have been farther from where I had started. It's hard to explain how I got to Irvine, or who I had become. It was less the result of specific choices than not making any.

But there I was, forgetting to vote in the gubernatorial race that elected Pete Wilson and only reading about current events if I accidentally turned to the wrong page looking for the movie listings. The closest I got to any spiritual fulfillment that year was finding a store at the mall that sold economy-sized bags of bobby socks.

There was no escaping it. I had become one of *them*.

Then the phone call. The growth on the mole was melanoma. There were no signs it had spread. *Not yet*. It was small. They may have gotten it in time. It may not be in the blood. It may not be in the lungs. It may not be in the liver, the pancreas, the brain. *Not yet*.

I got off the phone to face the concerned faces of my three roommates. *Insignificant*. That was all I could think of as I looked at them, at our pink stucco apartment in this planned community I lived in, at the life I had fallen into. *Insignificant*.

I went home to Washington for the surgery, when they excised a huge portion of her shoulder. The margins were all clean of cancer cells, but the level of invasion was borderline. They could not tell us if she was safe. At night, during the recovery, after my mother had gone to bed, I would sit in the living room under one small light, looking at old farm photographs and trying to remember what it had been like when everything seemed so possible.

The operation took place right before spring break so I stayed with her through vacation, until the incision started to heal. When I got back to Irvine, two-and-a-half weeks after I had left, everything had changed. It was as if those two years had been wasted time. There I was, part of a generation supposedly made up of dull-eyed, slack-mouthed losers, laughing at the stereotype, when, in fact, my mouth was so slack it *dragged*. I was twenty years old, living off my college loans, not learning anything, owned about nineteen baseball caps from the Gap and had absolutely no plans for the future.

But where did that leave me? There was something present in those photographs of the commune that had disappeared from my life, something that had been buried. Now, as I look at my headband and my white sneakers and my cute little socks and my pile of credit card bills, I don't even recognize myself.

My friends weren't any help. They took my sulking for average X-er angst. "Don't worry," they'd say helpfully. "Listen to Nine Inch Nails really loud for a couple of days—you'll be fine."

"Look," I would tell them, "my mother may be dying and my life may be meaningless and I'm tired of caring more about Snapple than political empowerment. Loud guitars are not going to make it better. All that loud guitars are going to do is make me deaf so that I won't be able to tell when all of you are ignoring me."

"Your point?"

I changed majors a few weeks later. Theater to political science, which, in a lot of ways didn't seem like much of a stretch, but was a source of enormous startled bemusement to my friends, and led to many encounters like this one:

"What's up?" My friend, Mike, had finally sat me down to find out what was wrong. We were at a coffeehouse with burlap bags stapled over the walls and two men playing dulcimers in one corner.

"My life is meaningless."

He looked at me and blinked. "No. Seriously."

"My-life-is-meaningless."

"Your life is not meaningless."

"How old am I?"

He sighed. "You're twenty-two."

"Do you know what my mother was doing when she was twenty-two?" He shook his head. "She was in Europe, with my father. He was evading the draft. Then they came back to the farm. She was running from the FBI. Protesting huge social injustice. Taking a stand. Living from her own vision. Do you know what I did today?" He shook his head. "I went to see a movie at the mall and then out to Cafe Armani for soup."

"You're not your mother, Chels. It's a different time. There's no war."

"There was."

"You mean the Gulf?"

"Yeah. What did you think about the Gulf War, Mike?"

"I don't know. I didn't have time to think. It was over in a weekend."

"That's exactly it. That's exactly how I feel," I said, "as if I don't have time to think."

"I think you're being too hard on yourself."

"What do we do for fun?"

"Huh?"

"What do we do for fun?"

"We come here."

"Okay, we go out for coffee. What else?"

"We see movies." I motioned for more. "We rent movies. We . . . we rent movies we've already seen."

"Uh huh."

"So what are you saying?"

I leaned forward. "My-life-is-meaningless."

I repeated that same conversation with several friends that year. All that changed was the coffeehouse. And they tried to understand, they did, but their notion of the sixties did not have the same origin as mine. The frame of reference they were working from was what they had gathered from the occasional *Hair* revival, not life. To them, the sixties were a greatest-hits collection on a late-night infomercial; Julie Christie in go-go boots; John F. Kennedy's head snapping forward in an Oliver Stone film.

But none of this had anything to do with what I was after. I wanted to be serious. I wanted to learn something. I wanted to understand what I was a product of. So I signed up for my first political science class, The Politics of Social Protest, and discovered that it was all about my parents. The readings were centered around the topics of my childhood: Kent State, the Chicago Seven, the demonstration at the 1968 Chicago Democratic Convention. I was thrilled, and still none of my classmates seemed to care. I quoted Mario Savio to a friend that quarter and he put one hand on each of my shoulders and shook me. "Hello? The sixties are over," he said. "For all our sakes, please, please, please *let them go*."

But those years were my connection to that woman sitting on the grassy hill next to my father. If I could understand that look of fierce determination on her face, I could understand it in my own reflection, and somehow keep a little part of both of us safe. But first I had to answer some questions.

So I did what any student faced with a big research project would do—I went to my college library. In my frantic zeal I must have read nearly every book they had that had anything to do with the sixties, including the three books on communes I found stuck in at one end of the communism section.

I thought if I read enough about the era I could somehow absorb what it must have been like, and if I could understand what it had been like, I could understand who my parents were and why it was so important to me to find out.

I explained this to my friends. "What do you mean by 'hippie'?" they wanted to know. "Do you mean someone who wore bell-bottoms? Someone with long hair?" (I could tell they were all envisioning Cher singing "I Got You Babe.")

"No, no, no," I said. "A hippie was . . . was—" And then I realized that I was in trouble. What *was* a hippie? The word wasn't even in my Powerbook's spell-check dictionary. Was a hippie simply someone who followed Dr. Leary's advice and "turned on, tuned in and dropped out"? My parents had done this. Politically they were very left. They took psychedelic drugs and smoked marijuana. They removed themselves from the Establishment. They didn't have drivers' licenses or Visa cards or bank accounts. They put together outfits entirely from patched denim. But there must have been other kinds of hippies, too.

The books I was reading didn't offer any new insights. They described hippies as disillusioned, middle-class white kids who used drugs to escape the Establishment's reality, and practiced free love to break down the repressive boundaries of a society that defined liberation as letting girls wear culottes in school.

In short, the books explained, hippies wanted to build a new society on the old corrupt one. They wanted to end the war, open minds and break down closed doors—they just didn't want to vote. This Catch-22 of revolution through non-participation was a source of endless debate among the be-spectacled sixties' sociologists, who were unsure of what to make of a social movement that didn't have a manifesto.

The books either wanted to make light of the hippie movement, or fit it into a complex political equation. The more I read, the more both angles seemed to be missing the point.

"We never called ourselves hippies—hippies is what other people called us," my dad once told me. "We were just trying to survive without compromising. We were trying to exist outside the war machine."

His explanation was clearer and more eloquent than anything I'd come across so far. Which made me realize that what I was reading in the UCI library had left a lot out. For the most part the books were academic, written by professors who had headed out to communes to study hippies like Diane Fossey tracking down gorillas. The books by people who had actually been part of the scene were so creatively driven, and in some cases drug-induced, that I had to look hard to find a topic sentence, much less a completed thought.

Most of the material reduced the sixties to dates, politics, music references and quotes. By the time I finished my research, I knew more trivia about the era than my parents. But in the end, all that information didn't bring me any closer to understanding what made us who we had been.

But I did have a foundation—a sense of what was at stake and for whom. So I started collecting my parents' memories to add to it. Tell me about the old cottonwood tree at the farm. Tell me about evading the draft. Tell me about running away to Mexico. Tell me. I envied their freedom, their adventures. I wanted to roll naked in the mud at Woodstock or protest something, anything. I mean, these were my parents, and their stories were better than any I could make up. "You've got to write some of this stuff down," I would say, to which my mother would grunt an amused dismissal.

"You do it," she would tell me. "You were there."

You were there.

She was right—but what part of that experience was still with me? My memories were vague at best. I remembered the dogs, my parents, the Snowqueen, the porch light. But they were images mostly, fragments of memories that, on the surface, had no real meaning. I tried to make sense of them. I examined every memory I had. And still none of it seemed to get me any closer to that little girl I had been, or to my mother.

My mother's medical saga, meanwhile, was continuing. That last year I was at UCI she was biopsied so many times that her torso was covered with small scars. None of the other moles they removed were melanoma, but the constant worrying was taking its toll on both of us. Sometimes, after a shower, I would stand naked in the bathroom slowly examining my skin inch by inch. Crushing my body near the mirror and straining my neck around, I imagined the cells in the moles on my back moving faster and faster. I could almost see the pigment darkening and the shape becoming asymmetrical before my eyes.

These passive attempts at self-reflection weren't going to cut it anymore. I had to do something. I can't even explain the intensity of that feeling—the innate instinct that I had to make a change.

Besides, this had gotten to be about more than just me. What I was trying to uncover involved my parents and the core values of the culture I was living in. It was about seeing if any of the old lessons I had learned were still relevant. It was about nurturing some little flame of my parents' passion. It was about finding some alternative to spending two hours a day sucking down espresso drinks at Starbucks.

If I was going to understand the hippie trip, however, it was going to be through my parents, not books, and if I was going to pull myself out of this funk, it was going to be through sorting out my own angst, not anyone else's.

Snowbird would be able to help.

But looking around at the five shades of pink in Irvine I knew that she wasn't going to be found lurking amongst the stucco and petunias.

I would have to go back to Iowa.

S nowbird is in the back seat, whistling. My
mother is drawing an Iowa corn goddess in
the trip journal and doesn't hear her, but I
recognize the song and turn to look. Yet the second
I turn around, the whistling stops. The back seat is
full of all my worldly possessions—no room for a
little girl. The only sound is the urgent scribble of
the yellow marker my mother is using to color in
the corn goddess's hair. Then I hear a whisper.

"Shhh!"

I jump, nearly swerving into oncoming traffic.

"Remember," a voice giggles from behind me,
"not to leave the tape on the door."

I whip my head around again. The cardboard
boxes stare back at me defensively. There is no sign
of Snowbird.

Remember not to leave the tape on the door. It is an old Watergate joke someone told me when I was a kid, though I don't remember who. I glance over at my mother. She is concentrating on the ears of the Iowa corn goddess.

As a child, I knew two things: that Richard Nixon was lying and that the system was corrupt. It took me a while to learn to articulate the second one. At the time I only knew that the system had tried to make my father fight in the war and that my mother wouldn't buy me products that were advertised on TV. From that I figured out two more things: that the system was dangerous, and that it was to be avoided.

I could do that on the farm. The other kids I knew were all hippie kids. We ran around naked, chasing the dogs and eating grass—we didn't need Barbies. I called my parents by their first names until I was nine. They didn't give me either of their last names because they wanted me to have my own. They listened to me. I had a say in family decisions. They wanted to raise me the way they wished they had been raised. I took baths when I wanted to. They never made me eat food I didn't like. They never lifted a hand to spank me. They explained why what I had done was wrong. It was an amazing experiment in child rearing, really. My parents did their best to let me be a kid without treating me like one.

But it was destined to end from the beginning, because it could never exist off the farm. The times changed, and the people changed with them. Twenty years later, no one gets the old Watergate jokes anymore, because no one remembers. Nixon dies and is lionized and Jerry Brown starts a commune for lawyers in Oakland. The Snowqueen, in all her free-spirited whimsy, hasn't been by to visit in seventeen years. And I don't even know if the farms we lived on are still standing.

Meanwhile, my father in his green felt Robin Hood shirt proudly wearing a button that says *immoral minority* and teaching me to sing peace songs to his banjo, has never seemed so young or so far away.

"But what do I have left?" I whined to him once.

He looked at me, perplexed. "Your childhood," he said.
Snowbird pokes me in the back of the head.
"Hey!" I whisper loudly.
She sighs.
What now?
But she doesn't poke me again.

My mother and I decide not to drive all the way to Pocatello and instead get off the highway about forty miles west, in Burley. It is dark and late and my mother has insisted that we drive around town for forty minutes looking for someplace "interesting" to stay before settling on the Econo-Lodge out by the highway. We check in, leave our things in the room and try to find a place to eat, but it is five minutes past ten and everything in Burley closes at half past nine. So we end up stopping at a grocery store where I buy a box of Banana Nut Crunch cereal, a fruit salad and a liter of mineral water, and my mother buys a box of crackers, cheese and a bottle of beer. We go back to the room to eat and I watch a special on the sinking of the *Titanic*.

This is what it's like traveling with my mother. She is a Buddhist and wants to "experience the place." I am an atheist and want to find the nearest, cheapest lodge with coffee, where I can sleep eight hours and then get back on the road. This slight difference in priorities has led to some discomfort in the past. My mother passes rest stops and wants to rest. I'd rather not make more than one stop per state. My mother gets hungry and wants to find a restaurant she likes and eat, I get hungry and want to go through a drive-through the next time we stop for gas. But this trip has been different. I think we have both been so lost in our own thoughts, that worrying about details—not to mention chitchat—has seemed incidental. That sort of thing is for tourists. We are travelers.

We still have a long way to go, though, so the next morning in Burley, we get up early, take showers, buy postcards in the lobby and then get back on the road, stopping briefly on the main drag to buy our third tank of gas and some bad coffee. The green and yellow hills are beginning to give way to tract housing and floral plastic patio furniture and we see fewer and fewer Oregon plates.

My mother, a tan baseball cap holding up her wet hair, opens the tin of Altoids Peppermints and offers me one. "The day hasn't started until you've popped your first mint," she says.

I take one, but it burns my tongue so I end up swallowing it with a bitter swill of coffee.

It is already hot, and we have the air conditioning on again. My mother, who does not seem to mind the coffee, keeps rewinding my Tom Waits tape so she can listen to "Heart of Saturday Night" again and again. I finally ask her to stop.

She sighs and leans her head against the side window, watching as the last of Pocatello gives way to farmland and irrigating spray. In the distance we can see the purple hills of Wyoming.

"What do you want to do first when we get to Iowa City?" she asks, for the sake of something to say.

I am quiet for a moment, thinking. "I want to find Donnie."

She pauses. "Well, we'll try, but we don't even know if he's still there." She doesn't want to discourage me, but we both know the truth: that Donnie was an alcoholic; that no one we know has seen him in years; that once we left, he was all alone.

We pass a truck ahead of us with an "I am the Way, the Truth, and the Life" sticker on the bumper and I keep my eyes on the horizon. "I'm afraid he's dead," I say.

She reaches over and puts her hand on my arm. A small, gentle touch, full of words. She is saying: "It won't surprise me if he is."

So there is the possibility of the unrecoverable. Donnie, the skinny, twenty-year-old farm kid who came to the farm for salvation, and when it all ended lost what comfort he had found; Donnie, who everyone loved but ended up leaving. He was the one who most embraced the dinner discussions of philosophy and politics; the one who spent the most time with me as a kid—helping me look for berries, grinning and whooping whenever we found one.

The closer we get to Iowa City, the more I want Donnie to be alive. Because if he is alive, then my past really is still there. If Donnie, the self-destructive, idealistic drunk, could survive, then so could Snowbird.

We drive awhile longer and my mother draws portraits of me behind the wheel in our trip journal. About noon we stop in Green River and decide to have lunch at the Cowboy Cafe because my mother likes the name. She orders a hamburger and fries for $2.90 and when it comes the meat is gray, the tomato is the size of a kiwi and the onions are too strong. I am smarter and order ice water and then stop at a Wendy's for fries on the way out of town.

When we finally get into Wyoming it is already dusk, and the whole horizon is layered with shades of violet. My mother produces a map we bought at a gas station. "Did you know that there are only four hundred thousand people in Wyoming?" she asks. "That's the same number as in Portland."

"I knew that."

She slides me a suspicious look and then goes back to the map.

After what seems like less than a second, without looking up, my mother asks: "What are you thinking about?"

And I say, "Nothing," more because I am tired of talking than because I don't want her to know. But she, I notice, is also quiet, and after a minute I wonder if she is thinking about Iowa too.

"Do you like to daydream?" Snowbird's father asks her one day when he is pulling her on a sled at the farm.

"Only sometimes," she says. "Sometimes, but not all the time."

*T*he old, white farmhouse had been built in 1889, and stood at the end of an unfinished lane that led into tall grass. There were four outbuildings—a big barn, a garden shed, an outhouse and a shed for the horses—as well as a side and front porch. Behind the house, off the yellow kitchen, stood an ancient cottonwood tree that had been there for a hundred years, or maybe two hundred, depending upon who was telling the story. On this particular day it would still have been summer, so the air would have been hot and humid. The breeze, if there were any, would be warm, rustling the leaves of the trees and sending the rusty weathervane on top of the barn twirling.

There would have been dogs asleep on the porch and two or three horses lolling in the pasture behind the barbed wire fence. At the base of the back porch would have been the vegetable garden—overflowing with tomatoes, beans, zucchini, cantaloupe, onions, basil and dill—and the corn in the field next door would have been green. But it would have been the old tree that impressed the young woman first.

"Look at that," she said, taking a breath and pointing it out to the young man she was with. They were driving up the lane for the very first time. The tree dwarfed the house and Mary folded her arms on the dash and peered up at it through the windshield of the red bus. "It's a cottonwood," she said. The young man nodded.

They were going to see Bob and Fern, who were renting the house, but were leaving for Venezuela (or was it Guatemala?) in a week and needed someone to look after it. The young man and woman had first lived in a little gray apartment in Iowa City when they returned from Europe in the fall, and then on a farm near Wellman. The first night at the farm they had a group of friends out to sleep under the stars and by morning every farmer in the area knew they were there. The young woman wanted to leave then, thinking that it wasn't safe, but they decided to stay.

A few weeks later, she discovered she was pregnant and was told to keep to bed. She spent the days reading while the young man made Spanish rice for dinner every night in the kitchen right next to the bedroom. The hog farm run by their landlord came right up to the edge of the house and it was a long time before the woman could stand the smell of pigs or rice again.

When Bob and Fern offered to sublease their place, Mary knew it would be perfect. Their farm was a good seven miles south of Iowa City. Close enough to hitchhike, but far enough out to get lost if you had to.

They parked the bus in the gravel driveway next to the run-down stable and climbed out into the heat. Fern came out onto the back porch, waving. Her long, gypsy hair was tied back at the neck and she wore a loose flowing dress. "A hippie queen," the young woman would later call her. Bob came out behind Fern. He had dark red hair and ruddy skin, and had broken his arm a few weeks before riding their horse, Rue. He was a short man, but he had the presence of a tall one.

Bob and Fern, who were a few years older than the young man and woman, had starred in porn movies in Los Angeles before coming to Iowa. Fern was from New York City and worked at the hospital, though no one ever knew exactly what she did there. Bob was from West Virginia and stayed home and gardened.

Fern opened her arms wide and gave the young woman a hug. "Mary," she said, "we were afraid you'd gotten lost."

Bob clapped the young man on the back. "Hey, man, come on inside. I'll get you a beer."

"I'm going to take Mary around the yard," Fern said, pulling Mary away from the porch by the hand. She turned to Mary, conspiratorially. "There's someone I want you to meet."

Fern led Mary past the rusted windmill, past the old cottonwood and down the hill toward the corn field. At the edge of the field a young woman was riding Rue. Her hair was long and blonde and she wore dirty overalls with no shirt. She rode the horse bareback, expertly controlling the animal's every move. When she saw Mary and Fern she rode up to them, stopping short a foot away from Mary. The horse whinnied.

"Shelley," Fern said, "this is Mary. She and Larry are going to take over the house."

Shelley grinned and reached a hand down to Mary. "Get on," she said.

"What?" said Mary.

"Get on." She held her hand down lower.

Mary looked down at her olive green minidress and tights. She looked at Fern. Fern smiled and nodded. Then Mary took Shelley's hand and climbed up behind her.

"Hold on," Shelley said.

Shelley gave Rue a quick, hard kick and the horse reared and started running. Mary stifled a scream. Rue kept running. Shelley laughed. Rue headed into the open field behind the house, and all of a sudden the three were jumping ditches and fences, while Mary squeezed her eyes shut and tried to remember to breathe.

"Open your eyes," Shelley yelled.

"What?" Mary asked.

"Open your eyes!"

Mary sucked in a breath and forced her eyes open. They were on a hill near the house, flying past poplars through tall grass. She could see Bob and Fern's farm. She could see the barn and the windmill. She could hear wild turkeys fleeing from their path.

Mary felt a whoop of exhilaration rise from her throat and out her lips.

Shelley led the horse back to the farm, slowing down to a more sedate gait. When they reached the back porch where Fern was sitting in the sun, waiting, Shelley turned to Mary.

"I'm moving in with you guys," she whispered. "When Bob and Fern leave, I'm going to move in with you guys."

She was true to her word. When Bob and Fern left a few days later, Shelley showed up with her husband, Curt, picked out a room and moved in. There was never any discussion about rent or why they had come; the event was simply accepted as any other that summer—without question.

Within a month, Elliott, a college friend of Larry's, came to visit with his friend, Randy. Elliott and Randy had recently finished serving their work time as conscientious objectors in Chicago, and, since they didn't have anyplace else they had to be, they ended up staying—Elliott in the house and Randy in his old, red camper truck, parked in the yard by the stable. The next week, Cunningham, another of Larry's friends, showed up with an army discharge for organizing against the war at boot camp, and took another of the bedrooms. Soon after, Donnie, the nephew of the woman who owned the farm, came for dinner one night and claimed the last downstairs bedroom, becoming the seventh permanent member of the household. Colleen, Mary's sister, and Colleen's boyfriend, Quinlan, and Tracy, would all come and go in the next few months, but it would be the seven who would make up the core group.

With all the guests came horses, cats, dogs, goats, chickens, sheep, marijuana and long discussions of the war and politics.

"We're going to move to British Columbia when we get enough money," Randy said. They were all sitting on the porch after dinner, smoking joints and drinking Pabst Blue Ribbon. Randy was explaining their plan to Patty, who had stopped by for the first time.

Shelley came up behind Curt and put her arms around him. "We're all going to live on a farm up there," she said to Patty. "All of us. We're all going to live on a farm at the end of a gravel lane four and five-eighths miles out of some little town."

"Four and six-eighths," Mary said.

Shelley was stoned. "We're all going to live in Canada, man, because in Canada you don't have to worry about the fucking draft, or Nixon, or Larry getting busted for resisting, and Mary's going to have her kid up there, because then it'll be a Canadian."

"What are you going to do up there?" Patty asked.

"I don't know. Arts and crafts or something. Or maybe we'll open a restaurant and serve vegetarian food."

"Oh. Cool."

Larry was sitting on the old mauve couch under the kitchen window with his hand on one of the dogs. "We're not going to go to Canada," he said. "We're not going to go to Canada because that would mean we'd have to leave here." But he said it so quietly no one heard.

"Tell me about your first date with Dad," I ask my mother.

She is driving and I have my feet up on the dash again. We're in Wyoming, heading into the last light of the sunset. It is going to be a cold night.

"He took me driving in a little green convertible that he'd borrowed. It started to rain and he didn't know how to put the top up. We got soaked. Later he cried about the children starving in Africa." She shrugs her shoulders a little, smiling. "I knew I was in love."

My mother was not born a hippie, like me. She was born a Mary, in a Catholic suburb full of Marys.

She slept with her hair rolled in brush rollers and wore plaid skirts and blazers with crests on the breast pockets. Her bobby socks were white and her hair was chestnut brown with bangs. She liked TV westerns, books with horses, reading *Seventeen* magazine and listening to Lettermen albums. She was going to grow up to marry a boy named Dave or Chip or Freddy, and live on a cul-de-sac with her Catholic babies and American car. She was going to vote Republican and play golf and drink vodka gimlets with other wives while discussing the latest dance number on the "Ed Sullivan Show." She was going to wear pantsuits and tease her hair like Tricia Nixon's and prepare meals from recipes on the side of a box of Hamburger Helper.

But this is not what happened.

Instead she discovered not what had been expected, but what could no longer be ignored. The myths of her childhood—the Red Scare, John Wayne in a G.I. uniform, refreshment bars that could double as fallout shelters—were replaced by realities she could no longer overlook.

The war was escalating. Student protests were becoming more violent. Bobby Kennedy and Martin Luther King were assassinated. Riots broke out at the Democratic Convention in Chicago. More students said they identified with Che Guevara than with any of the 1968 presidential candidates.

The effects that this escalating cultural turmoil had on my mother were enormous. For the Catholic daughter of a captain in the United States Air Force, the idea that individuals could step outside of and contest the system was both terrifying and liberating. She was forced to develop a political morality, not as an intellectual accessory, but as a social weapon.

My mother does not remember a distinct startled moment when she suddenly discovered her political conscience. It was not as if she was watching Walter Cronkite tally up the weekly body count on the evening news and suddenly thumped herself on the forehead. She remembers a girl on a school bus pulling out her guitar and singing a few Joan Baez songs. She remembers a handful of boys disappearing into the army after graduation. She remembers her father's complete and unquestioning support of the war.

But though her stray from the path to that Hamburger Helper box really didn't express itself socially and politically until college, the seeds had been planted much earlier. The repression and denial of her earlier life almost demanded that when she finally broke free, the snap would be loud and permanent. The mantras of her youth were a code of strict regulations. "Remember who you are and what you represent." "When you meet someone new, stand up straight, look them in the eye and shake their hand." I had the Snowqueen; she had saints. I had Lennon; she had Patton. To leave this, to abandon everything she thought her life would be, she had to leave it all. She had to surrender all her preconceived notions of marriage and family and flatware, and embrace a culture defined only by all it rejected. So she became a hippie.

This awakening started during her sophomore year at the University of Iowa, in 1967 and 1968. She grew her hair long and took to wearing Levi's with more holes than pockets. She smoked dope and dropped LSD and knew all the words to "Mrs. Robinson," which I would later find scrawled dutifully throughout all her college notebooks.

This rebellion against her former values certainly had ties to the war. Her identity had been closely wed to what it meant to be an American and when what it meant to be an American suddenly included napalm and mortar fire, her self-concept began to unravel. But it is important to note that her dive into the hippie culture was not a direct response to Vietnam, as was the case for my father. Rather, it was an escape from a whole system that had demanded, her whole life, that she be someone she wasn't.

A compliment my mother was quite proud of at the time came from a boy she knew briefly, who told her earnestly that he liked her because "she seemed like she was on acid, even when she wasn't." You have to know my mother to appreciate how funny this line is. She is a free spirit who my father, at his most disparaging, describes as "flighty." But her freedom and spontaneity come from a very serious place within that says, incessantly, quietly, this: be today, because you have it, and you may not have tomorrow.

There were moments when I was growing up when she lost this. She was raising me alone and working to get us through tough times. She did not have space in her head to consider taking an afternoon off and bicycling hard downhill just for the hell of it. But that changed when she was diagnosed with cancer.

After having the melanoma removed in 1992, my mother reevaluated her life. She sold our house and the garden nursery she owned in Bellingham, Washington, and moved to Portland, Oregon. After a two year bout with depression, she is finally on the mend.

I do not write easily about my mother's cancer. I am amazed by writers who are able to translate all that chaos and emotion onto paper. The hospitals and doctors, the constant phone calls from family members and friends, all too afraid to ask what they really want to know—these are the images I remember most. "How serious is it?" her friends would ask me, meaning, "Is she going to die?" But that's the thing with cancer: there is no telling. The diseased cells may be making their slow crawl across the shoulder, down the arm, into the lymph system, the kidneys, the lungs, the ovaries—or they may not. They work out your odds based on the size of the melanoma in relation to your number of cancer-free years. Under one millimeter + five cancer-free years = life. But the equations are for the patients; privately the doctors confess that there are always exceptions, even after a decade of remission.

Three years after the diagnosis, my mother is still alive. According to her personal equation, in five years she'll be home free. But neither of us has ever put much stock in math.

A few months ago she stopped going in for her checkups, and after initial qualms, I stopped bothering her about it. If

48

she doesn't want to know, then she doesn't want to know.

When she is in Mexico, I will tell old Iowa City friends who ask about her what she is up to. They will smile and nod as if they could not imagine her anyplace *but* Chiapas. To them, she is exactly who they remember—free, spiritual, adventurous. And I realize, finally, the connection. It has to do with danger, with a knowledge of the fragility of life. It is a knowledge that my mother had, too young, as a twenty year old, in the wake of Vietnam, and it is a knowledge that she would rediscover, years later, when confronted with the mutating cells of cancer. It is the first time I really understand the frantic vitality of what it must have been like for her to be young and politically alive in 1968. I understand now that she rejected the lies of her upbringing, not out of a lack of motivation or ambition, but a lack of time. As with her cancer, so many years later, she didn't have the luxury of reflection: she had to do, to be.

S he had to do to be.

Now it is my turn to try to live by this example. Starting with this trip back to Iowa, from here on in, I am going to exist in the moment, to Be Here Now. Because if we were all standing on the lip of the abyss in the late sixties, it sure doesn't seem as if we have taken any major steps backward. Those last few years in California, the universe seemed as if it might collapse at any minute.

During my sophomore year of college in 1992, a jury found the cops who beat Rodney King not guilty of excessive force and the corner of Florence and Normandy found its place in the American consciousness. I sat, an hour south of the chaos, in my carpeted apartment, riveted to the perfectly coiffed local news anchors' reports of "crazed gangs" and looting. That week Orange County gun sales skyrocketed and at UCI one thousand middle-class, white college students marched down Culver Boulevard chanting "No justice, ño peace," politely thanking the police officers in attendance for stopping traffic.

There were so many particles in the air from the fires burning in South Central that week that my asthmatic roommate announced one night that her lungs hurt and almost died in the car as I was driving her to the hospital. She was in the intensive care unit for eight days. Her health continued to deteriorate that year until she transferred to Cornell in Ithaca, New York, where she never had trouble breathing again.

Later that year a woman was killed by a mountain lion while jogging in a park in L.A. Authorities tracked down the lion and killed her, and then, a few days later, discovered that she had been protecting two cubs who were hidden in a cave near the public trail. They were eventually donated to a zoo in the Midwest.

It was also the year that, driving home from school one day, I noticed a mountain on the horizon that I had never seen before. I was in awe of the fact that, somehow, I had been missing this huge element of nature every day for three years, until I realized that this was the first time the smog had lifted high enough to see it.

Several months after that, at the beginning of my senior year, a six-point earthquake struck, panicking Angelinos—who were sure this was the Big One—and continuing to rattle the CD cases and all our nerves as aftershocks went on for months. Molly was on a ski trip with her sorority when it hit and I was all alone. Frightened, I called my mom and made her talk to me for a half hour, while I watched the glowing blue pool in the courtyard slop about and an apoplectic newscaster in Burbank send messages to his wife and kids to call the station if they were still alive.

Then, on Molly's birthday, the forest fires that had been

raging all through Southern California for the past week got too close, and our apartment was put on voluntary evacuation. Molly and I packed up garbage bags full of our most precious possessions (I saved my parents' record albums from the commune and family photographs; Molly saved her five pairs of Doc Martens), but at the last minute we decided to stay, watching through the kitchen window as fire crept over the hill only a mile west of us.

The fire receded and then smoldered, and the next day I used my college press pass to talk my way into the war zone that had been Laguna Beach. The hills around the beach town were black and the streets were crowded with uniformed National Guards and firefighters. The beach, where I had sat when life seemed crowded, was now covered with military helicopters, and reporters swarmed anxiously about, trying to find someone, anyone, whose house had been destroyed by the fire. The sign on the bank downtown read: *Closed due to unusual circumstances*. On the main street a Sparkletts truck was handing out free bottled water.

Then, as if nature hadn't been hard enough, that winter, heavy rain and flooding caused landslides in already fire-damaged areas in both Laguna and Malibu. Whole neighborhoods slid down hillsides. And in June, Nicole Brown Simpson and Ronald Goldman were murdered, O.J. Simpson was arrested and Molly accidentally slept through my graduation because she had been out all night with her boyfriend at a Hollywood club.

"You should have been here twenty years ago," a blonde woman with a two-carat diamond ring told me at a Christmas party. "Twenty years ago Southern California was a place to be." She had met her lawyer-husband at USC and they had lived in L.A. until moving to Oregon "for the children's sake." (Something about protecting them from the "illegal alien problem" or smog or something.)

She was right, too, in her own elitist, paranoid way. Southern California did seem to be nearing the eve of destruction.

Listening to the people talk, you'd think they had been warned by NASA that an asteroid was headed right for Laker Stadium and the estimated time of arrival was twenty-four hours. It was as if they had all been holding their breath for so long in anticipation of whatever next disaster lay in store that they were almost looking forward to getting it over with.

"Sometimes I hate it here," Molly said to me once. She was from Fontana, the crystal meth capital of California, where the head football coach at the high school made more than the superintendent of schools. Fontana is in the Inland Empire, east of Los Angeles, where the white flight first settled until the steel mills closed and those who could left and those who couldn't joined the local chapter of the Hell's Angels. According to Molly, there were days when the smog levels were so dangerous that the kids weren't allowed out for recess.

"Why don't you leave?" I asked.

Molly rolled her eyes. "Where would I go?"

"You could come to Iowa with me."

"Oh, right—Iowa," she said slowly. "Isn't that part of the big space you have to fly over to get to New York City?"

"Uh huh."

"Thanks, but I think I'll just move back in with my parents."

D o you see that red station wagon behind
us?"

My mother cranes her head around to
look out the back window. "Uh huh." It is dark and
we are the only two cars on this stretch of Wyoming highway.

"It's been behind us since Pocatello."

"The same one?"

"The same one. I recognize the ski rack."

She returns to the map she is reading. "Well,
maybe they're on their way to Iowa, too."

I shake my head. "Nope," I grin. "I think we're
being followed. Maybe it's the FBI. Maybe they're
still looking for you."

"FBI agents don't drive red station wagons. Besides, they found us twenty years ago. If they're still

looking they have even less interdepartmental communication than I thought."

I turn my blinker on. "I'm going to get off the highway and see if they follow us."

I pull off at the next exit, at a sign that promises gas, but no food or lodging. The red station wagon flies by down the highway, without even slowing to give us a second glance.

"They're good," I say.

"Come on," my mother sighs, pointing to an old Texaco station. "We might as well get gas."

I slide the car up next to one of the pumps, and hop out. The gas station is eerily absent of people, like Wyoming itself. There are no other cars. We are hundreds of miles from the next major town. There are no fast food places or motels, no place to get a Blizzard or a super-sized fries, no playground area for the kids. In fact, no kids. Beyond the gas station are miles and miles of deserted, fenced-off land, and beyond that, more land.

I stand there holding the nozzle in the car for what seems like an eternity, while gas leaks out of the pump into my tank. Above me the sky looks big and cold. I check the dials on the old pump, rattling the nozzle in a vain attempt to try to make the gas pump faster.

When the tank is finally full, I put the nozzle back on its hook. Before I can go inside to pay, my mother knocks on her window and rolls it down to push a few crumpled bills into my hand to pay for the gas and a bottle of mineral water.

"Mineral water?" I say, glancing doubtfully at our surroundings.

"Just ask."

I shrug, take the money and head inside.

The man behind the counter is as old as the universe.

His denim shirt looks as old and wrinkled as he is, and his hair is thick and white.

"Howdy," he says, not moving his mouth.

"Uh, howdy." I sound ridiculous. "Do you have, uh, mineral water?"

He sticks his thumb toward the right.

I follow it. "Thanks."

Somewhere in the building a light is flickering, giving the place a sort of black-and-white independent film feel, like at any minute El Mariachi is going to burst in and mow us both down in a hail of gunfire.

But he doesn't, and I am amazed to find a whole shelf of mineral water underneath the American beer, right next to a beef jerky display. I grab two bottles and take them back to the cash register. "These and gas," I say, putting a ten and a five on the counter.

He takes the money. "You heading east?"

"My mother and I are driving to Iowa."

"Iowa," he repeats. "Been there."

He hands me a dollar and change. "Keep your eyes on the road," he says, winking.

"Yeah," I say. "Thanks."

Arms full, I back-pedal out of the gas station and quickly make my way to the car.

I jump in and hand a bottle of mineral water to my mother, and she pops it open and takes a sip.

In a minute we are back on the highway. It is really dark now and I am unnerved by such a distinct absence of light. No headlights from other cars, no street lights, no houses or little towns, no glowing arches. It is like driving underwater.

Except for the stars. They are scattered thick above us, their constellations clearer than I ever remember seeing them. Though I can only name a few, I recognize others. I recognize the points and shapes and bright spots of constellations I have only paid attention to in books. These are Midwest stars. And as we get closer to Iowa, the stars get closer to forming the sky of my childhood—the sky that still sits over that old farm-house. I stretch my head forward to see more, and then re-member what the old man said and pull my attention back to the road.

I know that my friends think I'm weird for being so obsessed with what is so obviously over.
Chelsea, they say carefully, maybe you should
focus more on, oh, I don't know, the present/your
life/your future. They think I am like the boy in the
rhyme who refused to leave the deck of the burning ship out of loyalty to his father, the captain.
"Jump!" my friends yell. "Fire! Overboard!" But I
am more like the boy who does leave and then returns years later with Jacques Cousteau to lead the
salvage crew to the site where the ship went under.
I am like the submarine they send down to search
for a gold watch or a pair of men's spats on the ocean
floor around the shell of the ship's hull. But it isn't
the relics I'm interested in—it's the stories. And
even more interesting than that, the way we all

remember them.

For instance, my mother and father remember their time at the farm as differently as two people could. My father remembers people and events. He can tell you who was there and when and whose friend they were. He can tell you what stories were going on in the news in relation to everyday life, whether they dug the new outhouse before or after Kent State, and who had or had not yet been convicted for Watergate the day he rode out the lane on Rue after that blizzard of 1972.

My mother's memories are sensual. She remembers what was blooming in the garden, walking down the dusty gravel road to pick blackberries in the summertime, how big the moon looked at night from the porch. She remembers the clothes people wore, the stories they told and the summer the women all gardened topless ("on principle"). For a long time, when I needed details about the farm I went to my dad. I considered my mother useless when it came to names and dates. "I don't know when exactly that happened," she would say, "but the strawberries were ripe." But the more information I gather about that time, the more I realize that her memories are the most precious ones.

She was living in each day back then. The world, for her, was reduced to that old farmhouse and a few surrounding green acres. Time was measured by seasons, and philosophy and politics were expressed through music. What mattered was what was there: tending Snowbird, keeping the dogs from killing the sheep, keeping the neighboring farmers from shooting the dogs and making sure the goat got milked every morning.

No one at the farm had a job. They lived on food stamps, what they could grow and occasional odd jobs in town. Rent was paid by whomever had any money. On an average summer day Donnie would round up whoever was up and take a group into town to do some house painting. Those who didn't go to town would garden or do handiwork around the farm and then start dinner. My mom and Colleen might make millet casserole or tempura vegetables. Randy might make pizza,

Cunningham spaghetti. Elliott only made food that could be prepared over a campfire, which usually meant fried potatoes. At night there would be red wine and cold Pabst Blue Ribbon and everyone would sit around the long, oak kitchen table and eat and talk. After dinner they would drift out to the porch, smoke a few joints and continue whatever discussion had been started in the kitchen. "We talked about what our dreams were," my mother would tell me later. "And what our real lives were going to be like."

The next day it would start all over.

The life they created for themselves existed totally in the present. Cunningham, with his kerchief and banjo, playing union songs from the thirties to the fireflies; Randy, who knew how to live on nothing and was interested in everything (especially knives and engines); Curt, who loved Shelley even when she was at her craziest; Richard, another conscientious objector, who brought Mary her very first handpicked apple; Shelley, who once accused my mother of having me so she would have an excuse not to help with dinner; my mother's sister, Colleen, and her then-boyfriend Quinlan, a film student who would end up in medical school. Donnie and my parents. Patty, Tracy and Marta, and others who would come and go; Elliott, who once gave up a job because he thought it should have gone to a woman, and his girlfriend Krista, who would die tragically when she refused to seek treatment for a simple infection.

But it wasn't later yet, and for a moment they were safe from the swirling confusion of the outside world and required little interaction with it. Yet as idyllic as this seemed for a while, it was sure to break down. As expectations changed, one by one, my parents' friends left to pursue other paths. The war was over and they were all a little older, and I suppose it just seemed as if it was time to move on. By 1976, only the three of us remained. That summer, as I stood on the stairs, my mother would pack our belongings into brown cardboard boxes and tell my father we were moving into town.

~

Snowbird's mother is washing dishes and Snowbird is drying them with a dish rag and then standing on her tippy toes to push them onto the shelves.

"Why did you leave my dad?" she asks, realizing she doesn't know.

"Because he broke my favorite bread bowl."

Snowbird puts down the bowl she is drying. "Was it an accident?"

"Yes," her mother says. "It was."

"And you left him anyway?"

"Well," her mother considers. "It wasn't so much that he broke the bowl as it was that he didn't say he was sorry."

"Oh." Snowbird still hasn't picked up the bowl she had been drying. "Would you leave me," she asks, "if I broke your favorite bread bowl?"

"No," her mother tells her. "I would sell you to the gypsies so that I could buy another one."

11

"Oh, man," Shelley cried, "she's little."

"Hello, hello," said Donnie, poking a finger in the baby's face and wiggling it.

"Are we all going to name her?" asked Shelley.

Mary had just walked in from the hospital with the new baby. Dressed in the red velour maternity jumper she had made herself, long johns, boots and a huge down vest, she must have looked as if she had just popped outdoors to chop wood. Larry was unloading the car with Randy. Cunningham and Curt were probably getting beer. And Elliott had just put on "Tupelo Honey," the new Van Morrison album. *She's as sweet as tupelo honey. She's an angel in the first degree. She's an angel . . .* Even years later that music would still bring the little girl back to the farm.

They would all remember that first winter as being

the coldest. The wind blew almost constantly, blowing the snow from the fields into huge drifts. The pipes froze. Shelley, who had been sleeping in the hayloft for privacy, was forced inside, announcing one day at dinner that she would now be sleeping in the foyer. The dirt lane was snowed in, so that making it out every morning to the Donut Wagon for coffee had become a huge undertaking, requiring the driver to pick up speed on the hill, steer hard around a dip and then coast through an incline to the main road. If anything went wrong it would take the others all day to pull the car out of the ditch. That was also the winter the whole group took turns getting up during the night to start the cars in case Mary, who was nine months pregnant, went into labor.

On February 3, 1972, at four o'clock in the morning, her water broke.

Larry drove Mary safely out the lane in Cunningham's Volkswagen to the University Hospital, and on February 5, she delivered a little girl. Five days later, they brought their new baby home to the farm.

"Man, she's little," Shelley said again. Mary nodded, absently looking around the house. Someone had carefully draped old quilts and blankets over all the doorways. "What's all that?" she asked.

"Oh," said Shelley. "It was too cold in here for a tiny baby, so the guys did some chores for Florence and we spent the money at Goodwill on blankets to keep the draft down. Oh, and we planned the whole garden from some catalogs Elliott found at the unemployment office. We even cut out pictures." She produced a sauce-stained plan of that spring's garden.

Mary walked over to the living room where the wood stove was glowing orange and lowered her little girl into the walnut crib, a gift from Larry's parents. Shelley hovered. Elliott looked up from his place on the couch and grinned. "There's our little farm girl," he said. Larry and Randy finished unloading. Mike and Curt arrived with cases of Pabst. Donnie rocked the little walnut cradle. And through the kitchen speakers, Van Morrison sung about what mattered: love, friends, dancing and moonlight.

Three weeks later the little girl would still not have a name.

"Six weeks," her grandmother would tell her. "It was six." "We named you before we even left the hospital," Larry would say. But Mary made it clear: "Three weeks."

It was three weeks because it was early March. Still snowing. Mary was sitting in the rocking chair Shelley had donated, nursing the baby. Larry was asleep, but had been up to stoke the woodstove in the bedroom, which illuminated the room with a comforting flicker of light. The radio was playing softly and Judy Collins came on singing Joni Mitchell's song, "Chelsea Morning." The baby stopped nursing and smiled. She had chosen her name. "Chelsea," Mary said quietly. And because she had been born in winter— Chelsea Snow. The little girl would later take her mother's last name, Cain, and replace Snow with Elizabeth. But that was still years down the road. For now they would call her what they had from the beginning: Snowbird.

To the household's relief, spring came early. The pipes finally thawed. The cottonwood got its leaves. They planted the garden. As with chopping wood and digging the outhouse, planting the garden was one of the chores everyone was expected to help out with, and everyone did.

But besides this spring ritual, the routine was the same as always. The daily trip to the Donut Wagon stretched on for hours and afterward everyone would go into the Co-Op or work outside for a few hours and then, before they knew it, it was time to start dinner. There were always guests; friends of friends would stop by and stay for weeks. Family members visited, and people were always coming over from surrounding farms. Anyone was welcome, especially if they brought good pot or a case of Coors from west of the Rockies.

But it was all about to change.

Larry was the one who saw the list. He had gone into town for a few things and had picked up a Des Moines Register to see how McGovern was doing in the polls. The list was inside the first section and there it was—his name. Listed as one of the last five draft evaders from Iowa. They would be looking for him again. And he was so close.

Forgetting his errand, he got back in the car and drove straight back to the farm.

"Fuck Nixon," said Elliott. He and Larry and Cunningham were sitting on the porch. "It is all such bullshit."

"I'm not going." Larry was sitting on the couch under the kitchen window. "I'm not going to fight in that war."

Cunningham leaned toward him. "Just lay low, man. They won't find you. It's been two years. They think you're in Canada by now."

"He's right, Larry," said Elliott. "Just don't go into town for a while."

"What about Mary?" asked Cunningham.

Larry leaned his head onto the back of the couch and closed his eyes. "I'm not going to tell her yet. I'm not going to tell anyone. I don't want everyone to worry." He lifted his head up. "Besides, nothing will come of it, right?"

But a few days later, Larry found out from his parents that the FBI had started coming around again. Agents had even been out to Larry's grandfather's farm, which was only an hour up the road. They were close. Larry tried to stay cool, to avoid town, to think of anyone who might recognize his name and have a reason to turn him in.

But it was too late. A thousand feet of red tape were already rolling. The FBI sat outside Mary's parents' house day and night; they followed friends of Larry's who he hadn't seen in years. They knocked on his parents' door every day, so that even his mother finally stopped inviting them in. It was only a matter of time before they found him and Larry knew it.

Unsure of what to do, he took a chance and ventured into Iowa City to see a lawyer.

"Now let me get this straight," the lawyer said slowly, leaning back in his chair. He was wearing brown slacks, a wide brown tie and a pale yellow button-down shirt rolled up at the sleeves. Beside him a brown suit jacket hung on a hook over a brown cardigan. "You're living on a commune with a bunch of hippies, and the FBI is looking for you?"

Larry nodded.

"Son," the lawyer said—and Larry would remember his exact words—"you got to turn yourself in or the feds are going to deputize every redneck in the county and bust everyone at that farmhouse."

It is past eleven and we are on the highway outside Cheyenne—just us and about a hundred big rigs that all had parts in the movie *Maximum Overdrive*. Van Morrison is singing "Into the Mystic." My mother has fallen asleep, her head against the window, her mouth open. For a second I wonder again if she is thinking about Iowa, about my father—then I decide she isn't.

Above all else, I think it was my parents' separateness that always pulled me back to the farm, because it was there that we were last all together. From the moment we moved I was drawing pictures and writing stories about going back. It was the place where everything seemed possible, and in my mind it will always be exactly as I left it.

In my daydream I pull up to the old farm and

Sorrel runs out to greet me. She gallops to my side as if I've only been away a day or two and leads me inside. My father and mother are in the kitchen at the big wooden table. My father is young and strong, his blonde shoulder-length hair tied back with a bandanna. My mother is beautiful and healthy, her long brown hair combed straight and parted in the middle. They are laughing.

I don't want to interrupt so I slip past to look for Donnie and the others, and I end up in my old yellow bedroom. I sit down on my bed and remember the time my father taught me about light and how warm the red and green quilt was that my mother had stuffed with the cotton from her own baby blanket.

I am sitting on the bed remembering all this when Snowbird comes in. Her wild blonde hair is wilder than usual and her red dress is dirty. She sees me and stands in the doorway on the sides of her feet, the way that I still do sometimes, her hands in tight fists. She looks at me with her hard little blue eyes. Squints. Raises an eyebrow. Waits.

"It's me," I tell her. "I've come back to help you look for berries."

We try to get a hotel room in Cheyenne, but there is some big rodeo in town so every hotel room within a two-hour radius is booked. My mother stops at a cheap motel off the highway to ask the boy behind the counter if he knows of any place we can stay closer than Nebraska. He tells her about a dude ranch about forty minutes north in Centennial and we drive there in silence, exhausted and mad that we have to go so far out of our way.

We get the last vacant room and I am tired enough to go to sleep without watching any TV.

When I wake up eight hours later, my mother has already gone, leaving a note for me to meet her downstairs for breakfast.

The dude ranch, I discover in the daylight, looks like it was designed by Ben Cartwright, built out of logs and filled with the molting heads of dead animals. I find my mother sitting on the log porch sipping coffee and writing some postcards of jackalopes she's bought in the gift store. I am just sitting down beside her when nineteen bicyclists in brightly colored spandex jumpsuits and pointed helmets whiz by.

"Where do you think they're going?" I ask my mother.

"Who?" she says.

"You didn't see them?"

"Who?" she says.

"Never mind."

I smile. It's a metaphor for my adolescence—always pointing out something none of the other kids could ever see. After my mom and I moved, I suddenly found myself an anomaly. I was a hippie kid in a conservative middle-class town—sort of like being Dan Quayle at a Hemp Fest. I was six in 1978, when we left Iowa City for Bellingham, Washington. My mother had gone there to visit friends and we moved three months later. That fall she started school at Western Washington University to finish her B.A. degree in history and photography, and I started first grade at Lowell Elementary, the bane of my youthful existence.

These new lives we found ourselves living were startling. The kids at my school did not think about war and their parents were all married (I could tell by their matching sweater vests). My classmates all wore sneakers and jeans; I wore long, multicolored skirts, sweat socks and clogs. They had no idea how to deal with me, just as I had no idea how to even start to be like them. It was as if I was speaking another language. ("You're a trip," I told a classmate in third grade. "A what?" she said. "A trip." "A what?" And on and on.)

What I held on to those first years was 336 North Forest Street. That was the address—the first one I ever memorized—of the big white house we lived in. Originally built at the turn of the century to board the nurses who worked at a nearby hospital, it held a wonderful maze of rooms, hallways and sun porches. We had the two-bedroom apartment on the first floor. Upstairs were one-room apartments rented by students, except for two rooms rented by an old woman named Gertrude who had lived in the house as a nurse in the thirties and had come back to take care of her older brother, Ralph.

These people were my guardians. Whenever I caught the city bus home from school and had a few hours until my mom got home, I always knew that I could go to "the people upstairs" if I needed anything. Gertrude became my grandmother and the students who were always coming and going were ready friends. In that way a thread of the community of the farm continued through my childhood.

Those years, though, were especially hard for my mother. Raising a child alone while going to school full-time was tough work. She struggled with how much freedom to give me and how, somehow, to be true to both of us without compromising either of us. She was never the P.T.A. mom with pumps that I so coveted, and I was a fearless, spirited six-year-old who she had to remind "to leave a note" when I went out. But we talked. We talked about school and what we wanted to be when we grew up. We talked about books we were reading and friends we had and how we were going to travel to Italy. And we talked, again and again, about Iowa.

"I am remembering more about the farm," I say to my mother. We have checked out of the dude ranch and are heading back to the Interstate past the V Bar Guest Ranch and Big Hollow Road and we have to drive around a deer that was hit in last night's fog.

"Like what?" my mother asks, so I tell her about playing on the porch with the dogs.

When I'm done, she is quiet for a long time.

$\approx$

This is the riddle. You are traveling on a train. One evening you meet a man in a red turban playing mahjongg in the bar. (You have read too many Agatha Christie novels.) He tells you that you must get off at one of the next three stops. The first stop will be your past—the little English seaside town where you were born. Your parents, a fish monger and his wife, though long dead, will be there at the station. Everything will be exactly as you left it except that there is a chance you will discover a secret that could change everything you've ever thought you were. The danger is that you damage the memory, that by going back you destroy the past you've created in your head.

The second stop will be a bustling city in America. This is where you make your living as a newspaper reporter for a major daily. You left this place four months ago for your journey abroad. You left your job and your apartment and your hyperactive cat, but if you get off at the second stop you can have it all back, as if you never left. The danger is that you don't look back. You don't reflect. You don't have time to question the decision that brought you here.

The third stop is Vienna, the only stop actually on the schedule. Since Freud lives here it is perhaps your only hope for a carefree and productive future. The danger is that you've read *Dora: An Analysis of a Case of Hysteria,* and you've been fingering your purse a little too often to want to delve into it.

Or you can create a fourth choice—you can stay on the train. No dangers, no risks.

I knew an old professor at UCI who had escaped Nazi Germany as a twelve year old. His family sold their house for two pounds of butter to bribe a border guard with. He was eventually adopted by a family in Illinois, where he learned English, and tried to be an Average American Boy. A few years after he arrived, there was a knock on the door. It was his older sister. She had escaped the only way she could—by prostituting herself. But he was seventeen and an Average American Boy and did not want to be reminded of his past, so he told her to go away and never come back. She did. He joined the American army.

After the war he came back to the States and went to Harvard to study political science. He became obsessed with constitutional democracy, specifically how the Weimar Constitution was manipulated by Hitler so that he was able to commit all the Nazi atrocities without ever actually breaking it. He constructed his entire academic career around finding the loopholes that allowed this, hoping to prevent it from ever happening again.

In the midfifties, after he received his Ph.D., he decided to go back to the little town in Germany he had fled twenty years before. His family estate was now the Bureau of Tourism, and had been preserved exactly how his parents had left it when the soldiers came for them in the middle of the night. As he was standing in his old bedroom near the window where he and his sister had posed for the only photograph he had left to remind him of his family, a note was delivered to him. It read: *When you're done, come next door.*

He found his way outside the house to the small stone home next door. He knocked, and an elderly woman answered. It was his family's old housekeeper, the woman who had cared for him as a child and who had prepared the last meal he had eaten with his family before he had been smuggled away. She had made the meal again for him, down to the last bean and roll.

"How amazing! Did you go back again? Did you keep in touch with her?"

"No, no. I never went back. You see, I didn't have to after that. It was perfect. No matter how many times I went back, it could never be like that again."

My old professor had solved the riddle: he realized that nothing in the scenario dictated that getting off the train meant that you couldn't get back on again.

∾

My mother is drawing a jackalope in our trip journal and we get into an argument about whether they exist until finally I give in and we stop for gas. It comes to $4.99 with tax and we split it, leaving our postcards for the gas attendant to mail. On the way out we buy Bob Dylan's "Freewheelin'" tape from a rack for five dollars.

We listen to it over and over again until we get off I-80 for the night in Lincoln. (My mother has a theory that since Lincoln is a college town it will have vegetarian food and I have promised that a good meal of bean curd will cure me of my crankiness.) We weave our way through miles of construction and detours until, just when I am sure we've gone all the way through Lincoln and are about to pop out in, say, Kansas, we stumble across downtown. Lincoln is the biggest city we've stopped in so far on our journey, and after days of open sky and cows, I find it comforting to be surrounded by tall buildings. The main strip is several lanes wide with traffic, and because it is Saturday night, the cars are mostly filled with teenagers, hanging out the car windows and hooting at each other.

"Is this what Midwesterners do for fun?" I ask.

"When we're not busy dancing up a storm at the hoedown," my mother says, laughing.

"Do you knit your own plaid flannel?"

"Only the girls."

We get a room at a motor inn and claim our respective beds without arguing. Then, after changing into camouflage, we head out into the wild Lincoln night to hunt *falafel*, but find none and end up eating fries at a bar and going to bed early.

When Snowbird is still very small, her big doll, Linda, dies of natural causes. She carries the plastic body with the big head of matted red hair to her mother.

"Linda's dead," she says, propping the doll against the door frame.

"Well, then," her mother says. "We'll have to bury her, won't we?"

Snowbird looks at Linda. Linda looks back with her one eye. "Yes," says Snowbird, who has never been to a funeral.

Snowbird and her mother put on hats and gloves and winter coats and scarves and boots and go outside in the snow. While her mother trudges off to the barn to get a shovel, Snowbird sits on the edge of the porch with Linda.

"I'm cold," Linda says, her hard plastic body starting to shiver.

"You can't be cold," Snowbird tells her. "You're dead."

Her mother comes back with the shovel and the two of them find a place beneath the red elms and her mother digs a hole. The ground is frozen so it takes awhile to dig and Snowbird and her mother have time to talk.

"How did Linda lose her arm?" asks Snowbird. Linda had been her mother's doll before Snowbird was born.

"She was an astronaut and she was in a terrible space accident."

"Who gave Linda to you?"

"My father did. He came home from a trip to Germany in the middle of the night and when I woke up Linda was sitting in a box at the foot of my bed dressed like Heidi."

Snowbird is getting hungry and wants to go inside. Instead she asks: "Where is Germany?"

"In Europe." The hole is getting bigger.

"What was Grandpa doing there?"

"He was in the Air Force." Snowbird's mother finishes digging and lays the shovel beside the hole. Snowbird picks up Linda and hands her to her mother to set in the shallow grave. Together, she and her mother begin to push the frozen ground and snow in on top of the doll.

"How did Linda die?" asks Snowbird as her doll disappears from view. She isn't sad—she is certain Linda will be safe now.

Her mother pushes the last of the dirt in with the head of the shovel and pats it down with her boot. "She's been sick for a very long time," she says.

Snowbird is walking home from school when she sees the first of the dead birds. She is nine and in third grade and today she is walking home alone because she hasn't made many friends since she and her mother moved to the new state. But that is okay with her, because she likes to spend the time daydreaming anyway.

Snowbird has always collected things. Leaves, buttons, stamps, strange hats. Today she will start to collect dead birds.

She can tell the bird she has just found is dead because it is lying on the grass between the sidewalk and the street, wings clasped tightly to its sides, still and stiff. Its eyes are closed and sunken in and its orange-yellow claws are curled into tiny fists. There is a ribbon of yellow around its neck.

Snowbird picks up the bird without hesitation and puts the feathered body in her yellow Peanuts lunch box, carefully filling in the space around it with clumps of grass and dirt to cushion the jolting motions of the walk home.

She hurries back to the apartment and sets the lunch box on the counter in the kitchen. Her mother isn't home yet and the house is quiet except for one of the tenants playing the radio upstairs. She finds a shoebox in the basement and lines it with a bed of soft, pink toilet paper. Sitting on the floor of the kitchen, she takes the bird out of her lunch box, cradles it in both hands for a minute, then carefully places it in the box and seals the box with two pieces of masking tape.

It is before the first frost so the earth is soft and it doesn't take her long to dig a hole at the base of the dark red rhododendron bush in the front yard.

There is a short service, complete with a suitable black hat and a prayer to the Snowqueen, and then she positions the box at the bottom of the hole and fills in the cool dirt around it.

Her mother has told her the earth is made up of dead things, and that those dead things bring life to the living things, and she remembers this now as she packs the fresh dirt flat with her hands.

There are four more birds that week, all found on the way to or from school. By the second week the graveyard under the rhododendron bush has grown to seven.

She looks through the big picture book of birds that belongs to her mother and finds out that all the dead birds are evening grosbeaks. The next morning she gets up and walks to school early, stopping at all the houses on the way to inform the sleepy residents of the possible evening grosbeak epidemic.

At lunch recess she finds another bird, a crow, dead in the playground. She picks it up and wraps it in her jacket to take inside until she can bury it after school but the recess attendant sees her and tells her to put it down. She tries to explain about the evening grosbeaks, about The Danger, about the rhododendron graveyard, but the recess attendant's face is frozen in pinched horror and she just keeps pointing and saying "down, down, down."

Snowbird unwraps the crow from her jacket and carefully places it back where she found it. One of its wings is broken and flaps loosely down at the side of its body. Its neck is loose and bloodied from a scavenger that has been chewing on it and the black shiny feathers are matted with brown dust and bugs.

"I have to bury him," Snowbird says quietly, not looking up. The faces of the other children start to appear behind the recess attendant. One of them throws a stick at the crow. *Are you crazy?*

Snowbird keeps her head down. "I have to bury him," she says again.

She comes back later, after the final bell rings and school is over, but someone has taken the crow away.

Still the graveyard grows. Two cats, a chicken, a rabbit. She buries them all. Three more evening grosbeaks. She writes poems and reads them at the funerals. She invites the people who live upstairs and supplies funeral hats for everybody. Together, they bury a chicken, a kitten, a rabbit and a goldfish named Hue that the girl down the street had kept in a freezer for two years. She finds a dead cat by the curb. It is curled as if sleeping, only it has black bloodstains around its mouth. She carries it home wrapped in her sweater. It is a gray tabby and she buries it (and the sweater) across the front yard by the

holly bush because there is no more room under the rhododendron.

That red station wagon suddenly appears behind us again. I
am just about to point it out to my mother, when it speeds up
and passes us on the highway. In the second it flies by I catch
a glimpse of Snowbird in the passenger seat. She is looking
through a red plastic viewfinder and doesn't see me.

I glance toward my mother, who is asleep, and then back
toward the station wagon, which is quickly disappearing up
ahead of us, toward Iowa.

"Tell me what Iowa City will be like," I ask my mother
after the red station wagon is out of sight.

She rolls her head over and opens her eyes. "What?" she
asks, blinking.

"Tell me what Iowa City will be like." The corn fields of
Nebraska have given way to more corn fields and then even
more corn fields after that, so I have had time to wonder about
what I am going to find on the other side.

"You'll like it. It's a very progressive town. People come to
go to the university and end up staying the rest of their lives."

Beware all ye who enter here. "It sounds like some sort of
spell," I say.

"Well, some people leave," my mother says. "I did."

"We did."

We are quiet for a minute and I drum my thumb against
the steering wheel to the beat of a country singer wailing on
the only radio station in Nebraska. "What kind of radio sta-
tions do people in Iowa City listen to?" I ask.

"Oh, Iowa City is an NPR town," she says. "Definitely."

"How cold will it be in the winter? Will it be terrible? Will
I want to die?"

She grins. "Only between buildings."

I lean my head against the back of the seat while my mother
eats another mint. "These are the best mints I've ever had,"

81

she says. But I don't hear her because I am busy thinking about what it will be like to live in the town where Snowbird was born.

We get to eastern Nebraska in the early afternoon and decide to stop in the little town of Springfield, where my great-grandmother, Henrietta, a tall, blonde German woman, raised my grandfather and two great-uncles. Family lore says that her husband, my great-grandfather, was a bootlegger in Omaha until he was shot through the heart on the street and robbed. Henrietta moved back to Springfield after that, telling everyone that he had died of a heart attack, which, either way, I guess was true.

For the last few miles we have been listening to an oral history by Henrietta that my grandmother taped in 1980. My mother and I have been laughing because my grandmother grills her like an attorney, asking questions about her life as a girl, then challenging the answers. "Isn't one of your father's siblings still living—Rudolph?" "No." "Are you sure?" "They're all dead." "Well, then his wife is still living." "I said, they're all dead."

Now Henrietta, too, is dead, but my grandmother has given us directions to this town where she was born and raised. "Fifteen miles outside Omaha if driving east. Turn right at the truck stop with a giant teacup that says 'Sapp Brothers.' Five to seven miles."

The teacup turns out to be a coffeepot, but we get the point and abandon the highway for a two-lane road that leads into green hills spotted with white farmhouses. We accidentally drive by Springfield the first time and have to backtrack. The second time we see the sign and pull onto Main Street. There is a malt shop and a barber shop with a rotating red-and-white pole, and we sit in the car for a long time not wanting to get out and accidentally track dirt around or something. Then we remember Henrietta went to a one-room schoolhouse that is still standing somewhere near here and we go inside a dentist's office to ask for directions.

The curly-haired receptionist is thrilled and immediately telephones the local historian to inform him of our arrival.

"He's ninety-eight," she whispers to us. "It's all he has."

The receptionist puts my mother on the phone with the historian and he asks her a couple of questions and then gives her directions to the graveyard that contains our family plot. "Turn left at the statue of the naval officer. It's the wrought iron enclosure. Look for the Mohrs."

Then the receptionist, the dentist and three people waiting in the reception room for their check-ups tell us how to get to the old school and we walk two blocks right and one block left. But it isn't there. In its place is a brick school building that was built too late to be the one we are looking for. In the yard is a pile of wood and brick.

"Do you think they tore it down?" my mother asks.

"Maybe it's just the wrong school," I guess.

Undeterred, my mother stops on the way back to the car and asks an elderly woman walking into her house. From the sidewalk I hear her explain who we are and what we're looking for, and the woman, who tells us that she is Mrs. Herman Albert, beams and tells us to go across the street and talk to Mrs. Viola Schneider who went to school with my great-grandmother's little sister, Clara, and who still plays bridge with her every Wednesday.

Mrs. Viola Schneider comes to the door wearing a housedress, her bright, white hair wound up in a bun like an ancient ballerina's. She is tiny and shakes and when my mother explains to her who we are she flutters her arms up and down like a hummingbird.

She calms down after my mother offers her a mint.

"Do you know where the one-room schoolhouse is that Clara and Henrietta attended?" my mother asks her after we have made some small talk.

"Oh, yes," she says, and gives us directions. Left instead of right at the coffeepot. Highway 50 until you get to the Springfield Cemetery which is on the right side of the road. Road turns to gravel. Within one-and-a-half miles on the right side is the schoolhouse.

My mother writes it down.

"Have you been to see Clara?" Mrs. Schneider asks. "She's just up the road."

And, of course, we haven't because we weren't planning to, but Mrs. Schneider gives us directions and since they are so easy (straight ahead, next town, yellow house by park), we decide to go.

Clara's house is a Victorian, the color of warm butter, with a wraparound porch and a row of plump marigolds that run along the edge of the sidewalk. We knock and she comes to the door squinting.

"You're not going to believe this, but—" and my mother launches into who we are and the explanation is so familiar by now it seems as if her lips are moving around foreign syllables I can't understand. But Clara seems to and she wraps her old arms around us and holds our faces near hers so she can see what we look like, and I think I remember her from a family reunion at a Ramada Inn in Nebraska, but I'm not sure.

She leads us both into her living room. Everything in it is red—from the couch to the carpet to the lamp shades. Through a half open door I can see the guest bedroom and everything in it is pink.

"Sit down, dear," she says to me. Then she asks me about all my cousins, though actually she knows more about them than I do.

"Have a candy, dear," she says, thrusting a silver bowl full of bite-sized Snickers toward me.

And then, as I am forcing two into my mouth: "What are you studying, dear?" And I swallow half a Snickers whole and tell her that I want to be a writer and I can't remember, but am pretty sure, that Henrietta never called me *dear*.

Clara and my mother talk about relatives with names I don't recognize, memories of camping trips I've never heard about and what a card my grandfather was as a boy.

"You know," Clara quietly says to my mother, "you were always my favorite of Bill and Eileen's children."

After we have said good-bye and are in the car on the way to the old schoolhouse, my mother turns to me. "Clara is the one who inspired me to become a horticulturalist," she says. "She gave me my love of nature."

"How come you never talk about her then?"

My mother looks down at our directions. "It was a long time ago."

~

"What happened to your banjo?" Snowbird asks her father when she is nine. She is remembering how he used to play "The Swimming Song" and they would sing.

"Oh," her father says, looking down at his fingernails, "I don't have that anymore."

"What did you do with it?" Snowbird asks.

"I lent it to a friend and he never gave it back."

"Well, can't you ask your friend to return it?"

"It was a long time ago," her father says.

The schoolhouse that Henrietta and Clara went to has been abandoned since the thirties and the grass that surrounds it is tall and green. The porch that once stood in front has caved in after half a century of neglect, but the main structure still stands, a tribute to the pioneers and my great-great-grandfather who helped build it. My mother and I pull the car to the side of the road across from acres of corn field and barbed wire fence and work our way through the tall, green grass and over the porch and then through the opening where the front door used to be.

Inside is a main room where a few old desks still stand in the corner, rotting. Part of the roof has caved in so the wooden floor is layered with boards and rusty nails and we have to watch where we step because the floorboards are unstable. But I am amazed at what remains: a blackboard hanging on the far wall, warped and cracked, a few iron hooks in the old cloakroom, some pieces of thick glass bottles in the pantry.

We look around a little more, and then go back outside into the sun where I find a board with white paint on it in the grass. I pick it up and turn it over in my hands—a piece of my history. I bend to return it to the grass, but then I change my mind and decide to take it with me.

～

After leaving the school, we follow the old historian's directions to the cemetery, where we find the Mohr plot just to the left of the statue of the naval officer, exactly as he said. According to my grandmother, the wrought iron gate around the plot was cast and molded by my great-great-great-grandfather, Henry Mohr, Senior, who came over from Hamburg during the Civil War.

The area around the cemetery has been developed right up to its edge and the tall, brown apartment buildings across the street and on all sides make the graves feel small and out of place. Henrietta said that when she was a girl the cemetery was surrounded by green fields and took twenty minutes to get to by horse and buggy on dirt roads. Now the sounds of traffic from the highway scare away the birds.

There are twelve graves in the Mohr plot with one headstone reserved for Clara, her name and birth date already inscribed, the date of death left vacant. Her husband is buried here, along with her parents and her grandparents. She had told us that she comes here sometimes in the mornings, and I think for a long time how very strange it must be to visit your own grave.

My mother copies down the names on the stones into our trip journal: J. Henry Mohr, Elise Mohr, another Henry, Mary Elizabeth, Anna, Herman, Marie. How many of them died of cancer?

Louise, Albert Sass. A third Henry. Good, solid Midwestern names of people who lived their whole lives before I was born. People who canned tomatoes in summer kitchens and rode in buggies and went to school in one-room schoolhouses. Tall, stubborn blondes with my ears and pointy knees who are now long buried, their lives marked with worn little gravestones in a cemetery surrounded by tract housing.

My mother points to a grave. "Mary Elizabeth," she says. "I was named after her."

Driving back to the highway, the corn looks the exact color of a yellow Post-it pad. The road is gravel. The houses are all white. My mother and I stare out the window in quiet contemplation until, even though we already have heard it all, I put Henrietta's tape back in the cassette player, just to hear her voice.

A few months after Snowbird and her mother leave the farm, Snowbird's father leaves the farm, too, and moves into the apartment below theirs in Iowa City. He brings Sorrel with him. Snowbird likes this because, for a few months, she and her mother and father and Sorrel and Donnie all live in the same house and it is almost like being at the farm.

But Sorrel is a country dog. She likes to run fast and wild and chase coons and be around lots of other dogs. In the city she sits by herself on the porch looking sad, as if she is remembering better days.

So one day, Snowbird and her father and Sorrel go for a ride in the country to a farm where some friends of her father's live. Snowbird's father already has explained to Sorrel and Snowbird that this is what is best and that Sorrel needs a place to live without dogcatchers or cars, but all three of them cry anyway.

They go back and visit a few months later and Sorrel bounds over to them because she still remembers riding in that blizzard and long walks on the farm and what it felt like to carry Snowbird on her back. She bounds over and Snowbird and her father scratch her head and play with her and then they say good-bye again and ride back to town in Donnie's truck.

"Why are some of Sorrel's teeth gone?" Snowbird asks her father on the way.

"Because," her father tells her, "Sorrel is getting old."

Even after Sorrel is gone, Snowbird still likes to go to the grassy park where they used to walk her, and it is here she finds her boots. She sees them sitting alone on a park bench and she knows immediately that they belong to her, so she takes them home to the blue house where she lives sometimes with her dad and lets them dry out on the porch in the yellow sunlight that floats across it in the afternoon.

When the boots are dry she slips the fading brown vinyl over her wiggling toes and dances a waltz around the porch, liking the sound her feet make on the wooden planks. Then she jumps up and down and hops on one foot and spins around and around in circles until the brown gives way to cherry, Wonder Woman red and the vinyl to leather, and the lining that is thick with mold feels soft like silk.

The boots are her strength that year. They protect her and teach her a most important lesson—to be true to the stories that live in her head. And she can run faster and skip higher and kick harder in those boots than anyone else in the whole world.

Then, when they move away from that place to another state that has mountains and a deep, dark blue ocean, she begins to notice that her boots are not so red anymore. She has other things to do and the boots seem dirty and begin to smell like old things. She doesn't remember throwing them out or taking them to Goodwill, just realizing one day that they weren't around anymore.

She misses them sometimes.

But she can still remember how fast her heart was beating when she first saw them and how she and her dad took turns carrying them home that night, and sometimes, when it's quiet, she can still hear the hollow thumping sound they made on the porch of her dad's blue house.

It is an important lesson, and she will remember it later: just because you don't still have something doesn't mean it is lost.

In the summer of 1980, Snowbird sits on the beach in Key West, Florida, and watches the boats full of Cuban refugees come in. They are part of the Mariel boatlift, each one trying to make it past the big Coast Guard ships to the beach, so they can lose themselves in South Florida. Her father has moved to this place with a woman he loves and her son. They are Snowbird's summer family, and she will spend many hours with them playing in the ocean and sitting on the balcony waiting for the evening breeze.

On this day, she and her father have ridden their bikes with the wire baskets attached to the handlebars to the docks to watch the sunset.

They leave the bikes (you didn't need to tie them up back then) and walk down to the sand and she takes off her blue flip-flops (five dollars at Fausto's) and carries them so she can feel the warmth beneath her feet—callused and hard from a summer spent barefoot.

They sit on the edge of the Atlantic and watch the dark orange sun sink into the ocean, leaving behind one small boat weighed down deep in the water by too many wet, desperate bodies. They want to escape their old lives, her father explains to her, and find a better place.

When the boat is about one hundred yards offshore and the waves are so high above the bow that the whole craft seems to disappear from view, the passengers start jumping. Brown, half-naked, sun-baked bodies diving into the salt water, and then swimming, above and below the water, riding the waves to shore.

There was a strict policy in those days for residents of Key West to report refugee boats to the Coast Guard so that the crafts could be intercepted and the passengers scooped up and taken to internment camps for processing. But Snowbird and her father are the only ones on the beach that day. The air is full of the sweet smell of the sea and the game fish hung up on the dock by the season's few tourists.

Silently, she reaches beside her and puts her small hand on her father's larger one.

"What should we do?" she whispers.

He looks out at the ninety miles of sea before them. Days of sweat and thirst and heat and hope. And he says to her, "Nothing."

And the two stand up and walk back to their bikes with the wire baskets attached to the handlebars and by the time the first man or woman makes it to dry land they are pedaling back down Duval Street, he riding just ahead of her but slowing every so often so that she never gets far behind.

This is how I like to remember my father: riding his old metal bike barefoot, his long beard covering his bare, tan chest. The night I graduated from high school, I asked him when he had felt the most a part of history. He said the time he was tear-gassed while demonstrating against the war in Chicago, and that night he sat with his daughter and watched the Mariel boatlift come in. Of course I pressed him about the commune—if any of them ever felt the significance of their experience—but he simply shook his head and smiled.

"We were just a bunch of friends," he told me once, "coming from different places and trying to get by."

I have asked my mother the same questions: Why are there no group photographs? Why didn't anyone take more trouble to document their time on the farm?

She just looks at me sideways as if she is trying to figure out how I could possibly be her daughter.

"We weren't there," she told me once, "to be a layout in *Life* magazine. We were there because we each didn't want to be someplace else."

We are just getting out of the car at a rest stop in Nebraska, when the windstorm hits. Clouds roll in like mud kicked up in a pond, and the trees and fields bend under the strong gusts.

"What should we do?" I ask my mother, but the words blow past her.

She points toward the small brick building where the bathrooms are and we run toward them, laughing, unable to imagine that we are here, at a rest stop in Nebraska, in a windstorm. There are several other women standing just inside the door. They are Nebraska women—wearing blue jeans and cotton shirts, their hair in ponytails. Ranch women.

"Hey," one of them says kindly, flicking some

ash from her cigarette into the wastepaper basket. "You heading east?"

"Yep," my mother says.

"Storm's moving west," the ranch woman explains.

Outside a thick swirl of dust obscures the landscape. More cars are pulling off the road. "Should we move to the center of the building or something?" I ask.

The ranch woman slides a long look at another ranch woman who has been listening. The second woman raises both her eyebrows and glances at me like I am a dull-witted but good-natured calf, and says: "It'll pass."

It does in a few minutes. The wind stops short as if someone suddenly remembered to close an open window, the dust clears, and all at once it is sunny and hot again. The women climb back into their trucks and get back on the road. We follow, climbing back into the Honda, still a little in awe. We don't remember that we had to use the bathroom until we are a few miles down the road.

Hours later, my mother is still talking about those lean ranch women throwing up dirt as they roared away in their Fords and Chevys. They are the kind of women she imagined being once, when she was a kid and wanted to grow up to be Belle Starr. The trouble was she lived in a world that expected Sandra Dee, or at the very least, Miss Kitty.

When her father was reassigned from Bermuda to the States, she thought they would all move to a ranch like the one Roy Rogers lived on. But America was not Out West and the family moved to a suburb outside Chicago, a city my mother remembers as being filled with cars that moved much too fast. She didn't give up her Western fantasies, though, and every week on the way home from school she would stop at the dime store to buy a big bag of cowboys and Indians for $1.69. She doesn't remember playing with them, or even opening the bags, just placing them in a special box she kept under her bed.

One day her parents announced that they were all moving to Levittown, New Jersey, a planned community with Tudor, colonial, and ranch-style houses and a big club house swimming pool. My mother wanted to move into a ranch-style, but the rest of the family, who had always preferred "Father Knows Best" to "Rawhide," won out, and they moved into a colonial, with a shrub on either side of the front stoop. Everyone was happy with the big yard and the mall down the street, and if her parents knew that Old Man Levitt only sold houses to white people, they didn't seem to mind.

The nearest ranch-style, just a few houses down the street, was owned by a couple with two Pomeranians and a brand-new Cadillac who were always yelling, "Don't touch that car!"

That summer my mother taught her neighbors' dogs to jump through a hoop and in the fall started seventh grade at the big public school. On the first day of class she wore a fitted olive green skirt, a blouse with olive green polka dots on a white background and nylons. Her mother had given all the girls home perms the night before and on the way to school my mother caught sight of her shadow on the pavement.

"God," she remembers thinking. "I hope that's not me."

Later they would move to a big house in Longmont, Colorado, with spruce trees in the front yard that bats would fly in at night.

This is my mother as a ten-year-old: sweet, round face, knee socks, pug nose. Until she was a teenager, her favorite movie was *Old Yeller*. I hold up a photograph of this pixie-cut adolescent next to the photograph of my parents on the hill, and at first glance there is no correlation. This ten-year-old is all bangs and dimples and straight lines; my mother is all wild, beautiful abandon. But if I look closely at the second photo, I can still see some of that ten-year-old's longings. I can still see a glimmer of her Original Nature. When you think about it, her ending up on a hippie commune wasn't so out of character at all. She is the little girl who never got to live on a ranch, who grew up to live on a farm.

My father's parents were both from Clinton, Iowa, but his mother had been a W.A.V.E. during World War II and had driven buses at a marine base in South Carolina, and his father had enlisted in the Navy and was stationed on a battleship in the South Pacific. His parents were courting all through the war; his father would send his mother handsome photographs of himself standing bare chested on deck, hands on hips, an unfiltered cigarette hanging out of his mouth. My grandmother kept every photograph and they were married as soon as the war ended.

My grandfather, a big man, used to stand in the front yard and let my father and his brother jump off the second story into his arms. They played this game for a few years, from the time my father was about six, until one day the neighbor lady happened to see my father plummeting through space outside her open window. She screamed and my grandmother put an end to it.

My grandfather was also a strong man and the worst threat my grandmother could make was, "Do you want me to tell your father you said/thought/did that?" But he always came through when his kids needed him, like the story my dad tells about the day he broke two windows. My father was playing baseball in the alley, which was off-limits, and first broke one of the windows in his own house. That same afternoon, he broke one of the windows at the neighbor's. My grandmother called my grandfather at the fire station where he had been working a twenty-four-hour shift. "Larry has something he wants to tell you," she said, handing the phone to my father. My dad shakily explained what had happened. There was a long pause. "Well," my grandfather said finally, "it looks like you had a good day at the plate."

Years after, when the FBI would come every April and

October to my grandparents' house looking for my father, my grandfather, whose brother had spent two years in a Japanese prisoner-of-war camp, would look them in the eyes and lie.

Later my father would teach me how to fold pants the way his father had learned in the Navy: lining up the cuffs and then folding them over a hanger to create deep creases.

For my father's family—working-class Democrats—the idea of being anti-war was more acceptable than for my mother's. His family was Catholic, after all, and as long as there were figures like the Berrigan brothers to make fighting against the war holy, it could be tolerated. Evading the draft was another story. My grandfather was in the Navy for eight years—he even had a tattoo to prove it. When your country needed you, you went. It didn't matter what your politics were. It was only after watching the coverage of the riots at the Democratic Convention in Chicago that my grandparents finally understood. When they saw young people their children's age being billy clubbed by obscenity-hurling Chicago cops on the evening news, they knew their son was on the right side.

J ust short of the Iowa-Nebraska border, my
mother wants a sandwich, so we stop at a diner
off the highway. It is one of those places that
is about six-hundred watts too well-lit, with red
vinyl seats and a beverage list that offers "orange-
flavored drink" instead of juice. As we walk inside
I remember reading about a scientific study in
which intensive exposure to fluorescent lights was
found to cause insanity in rats.

My mother, of course, loves the place, claiming
happily that it is "perfectly Midwest." I follow her
over to the far side in the back and we take a place
at the pink formica counter, next to, as it turns out,
the local sheriff. He and my mother immediately
strike up a conversation.

The sheriff: "Where you all headed?"

My mother: "We're just passing through. I'm driving my daughter back to Iowa."

The sheriff: "Been to Walnut?"

My mother: Blank look.

The sheriff: "Walnut. Door-to-door antiques. Just bought myself three hundred lunch boxes for three hundred dollars at an auction there. Already resold one hundred of them for twenty-five hundred dollars. Davey Crockett alone went for four hundred."

My mother: "You collect lunch boxes?"

The sheriff: "When I can get them. Sold a Bionic Woman for two hundred, but westerns usually sell best."

I am thinking now of my yellow Peanuts lunch box in my mother's basement and trying to remember if I still have the thermos. The waitress delivers my mother's club sandwich and fries and, after I remind her, my ice water, and my mother starts to eat and continues talking to the sheriff. I think that, after three days in the car, she is simply happy not to be talking to me.

"Yep," he is saying, "I started working for the police department fifteen years ago when I was twenty-one as a part-timer. Needed the money, see. Don't do much, just bust kids drinking in the corn fields, mostly. Hadn't realized I'd been doing it so long until the city told me last week I'd saved up four weeks' paid vacation. It's a job though." He eats his last bite of cherry pie and the waitress slips his check under his plate as she does once a day, every day. "You all really should stop through Walnut," he says, ignoring the check. "It's on your way. If you don't stop, you'll be missing a real opportunity."

When we leave, he is still sitting there.

My father smoked pot every day for five years. He tells me this when I am fourteen and we are riding in his Jeep in Florida. Of course I already know; my mother has told me the story of how they had to harvest the marijuana early one season because my father's probation officer was coming to the farm. They finished just as he pulled into the driveway, but in their hurry someone dropped one stalk in the front yard and my mother had to distract the officer while Donnie scurried it away.

My father smoked pot every day for five years. He is telling me this because he wants me to know he now regrets it and that while he was using it he didn't want to do much else. He wants me to know, so I will remember when I am first offered a joint and will think twice about taking a hit. *My father smoked pot every day for five years.*

I don't tell him that my mother still smokes pot occasionally or that she has already told me that if I ever decide to get high she wants me to get high with her.

"I don't want you to use drugs," she tells me when I am thirteen. "But if you do, don't ever buy drugs from someone you don't know, don't ever use them with someone you don't feel safe with and if you ever feel like you are in an unsafe situation, call me."

In the end, I didn't end up getting high until college, and then I called my mother the very next day. I can't say that she was proud exactly, but she was amused and pleased to be let in on the experience. To this day drugs are a topic I never shy away from with her. I don't think marijuana is harmless—I have friends who smoke it way too much and you can almost see their brain cells leaking out through their ears. But then I've signed the California Hemp Initiative something like seven times, so I don't think it's the dark plague they tell you about in high school either. As for other drugs my parents took, like LSD and mushrooms, I tried those, too, in college, and they were interesting, but didn't hold my attention— probably because my parents allowed me to learn from my own experiences, rather than theirs.

18

My parents, too, learned from experience. They didn't come to that farm commune accidentally. The journey there was made up of a thousand steps—both small and large events that led them to no other possible destination. They were not only products of their time, they were products of their own histories. In the end, as with so many of their generation, being antiwar was not a political stance, it was a personal one.

These are some war stories my parents told me:

1) The Arrest. My grandparents had decided to send my mother to Estes Park, Colorado, for the summer, even though she had worked for months saving money so that she could spend the summer

in Provincetown with her roommate, Priscilla. But their plan was foiled. During a four hour stand-by wait in the Denver airport my mother met a young man named Mark who looked exactly like Jean Claude Killy and had once published a photograph in *Life* magazine. He offered to drive her the rest of the way, and after spending a few days with him, my mother decided that a summer with Mark looked a lot better than a summer in Estes. They lived in Snowmass for a few months and then ended up in San Francisco with a bunch of Mark's friends. One day another friend of Mark's called from Denver. He had come across an article in the newspaper about this wild marijuana that was growing around the Nebraska State Penitentiary. Wouldn't it be funny, the writer of the article wondered, if someone tried to cut it down? Mark's friend thought this was a terrific idea, and convinced Mark and my mother to get in on the action. A few days later they had a buyer and were on their way to Nebraska. Of course they were arrested almost immediately, machetes in hand, and that night their faces were all over the evening news. Crazed Hippies Harvest Hemp. Henrietta was living in Nebraska then and when she saw my mother in handcuffs flashing a peace sign on the six o'clock news she immediately called my grandfather, who was just sitting down to dinner in Davenport, Iowa. He drove to Lincoln and bailed my mother out of jail the next day. After the hearing, she never saw Mark or the others again. A few weeks later she got a call though. It was from Mark, phoning from jail. "The gig's up," he said. They were sending him to Vietnam.

2) The Accident. In the spring of 1968, my mother drove to Mexico with her boyfriend, Dick. He was running from his parents and the draft—she was along for the adventure. Dick's drug use kept escalating though, and my mother soon realized that his LSD and pot use was getting out of control. One day, when he went in to use a bathroom in a cantina in Mazatlan,

she asked if there was anyone there who could give her a lift back to the States. Dick heard her and came storming out of the bathroom in a rage, announcing that he would drive her back and that she didn't have to get a stranger to take her. They got in his cherry red VW bug and started to head north, only he wanted to get high so my mother had to drive. Angry at Dick for his outburst, she was going way too fast, and they hit gravel on a bridge. She woke up on her back in a field staring up at the sky surrounded by concerned looking Mexicans. Dick was lying next to her and she thought he was dead. They were taken to a hospital where the doctors told my mother that she had a broken collar bone. Dick, they told her, had a broken hip and was lucky to be alive. He had to stay in the hospital for a month and my mother stayed with him. Eventually, my grandparents sent my mother a ticket and she was able to fly home. Soon after, Dick's mother came down and flew him back to New York. My mother heard later that his broken hip had gotten him out of the draft. But just two years later, she would face the same angst all over again with another young man—my father.

3) The Suspension. In December of his senior year, my father was almost expelled from his Catholic high school. There had been a dance and a friend of his had taken orders for beer. It had been done a dozen times before—you wrote down what you wanted, gave him money and then he had it waiting for you in the trunk of his car outside the dance hall. My dad ordered a six pack, but basketball practice ran over and by the time he and one of his teammates got to the parking lot, the beer had all been given away. The next day word of the drinking got to the priests and they called in my dad's friend who promptly surrendered the list of names. There were ten names on it, including my father's, and all ten boys were immediately suspended. My dad and his teammate—because they were on the basketball team—made the front page of the local

sports section, and soon the whole town knew. After ten anxious days at home wondering if he would be expelled, the school announced that all the boys on the list would be kicked out, except my dad and the other basketball player, since they had never actually received the alcohol. (And probably because basketball was supposed to go to state that year.) The other eight boys were expelled. Some were athletes, football players—they were all good friends of my father's. The only other high school in town was the public school that had been their arch rival. A few swallowed their pride and went, the other three took the only other option they saw available—they shipped out to Vietnam. Of the two my father kept track of, one was killed, and the other had a breakdown and ended up in a V.A. hospital in Colorado.

My dad graduated in the spring, and in the fall went off to college. He returned to that town twice. Once, when I was a baby, to take me to visit his grandfather, and then again, a few years later, for his grandfather's funeral. Other than that, he never looked back.

I can see Mary now, leaning back in the orange vinyl chair, her eyes closed. Dick, Mark—so many boys whose lives were shaped by the war. And now Larry. She had always known, of course, that there was a chance they would have to face a trial. But she never let herself believe it would come this far. She had really believed they were safe. Now everything they had created was beginning to unravel.

She snapped her eyes back open. Focus. She and Larry were sitting in Preston Penny's office. He was the trial lawyer that the first lawyer recommended—he had once heard Penny say something controversial at a bar association meeting. His office, fortuitously enough, was located one block up from the Donut Wagon.

Penny was a big man with thick, dark hair, a bushy brown mustache, and a penchant for dark, three-piece suits. As Larry was classified as indigent, Penny was paid by the state, so the case was not high on his priority list. But he took to Mary right away and agreed to do his best.

Larry would have made the announcement the night before, after dinner. It was the summer of 1972. One of those hot, humid nights when the fireflies would have come out from the corn fields and just sort of hung in the air.

They would have all been on the porch: Mary, Larry, Snowbird, Donnie, Elliott, Cunningham, Curt and Shelley. Dinner would have been fresh from the garden, probably tomato pasta or homemade soup. Larry would have said what was on his mind, quietly, as if he were announcing a plan that had been made, and was his to make, as it was his to live with. After the decision to resist the draft, this was the second biggest he'd ever make. He would turn himself in.

The newspaper article, the FBI's new interest in family members and a phone call from Mary's mother saying that the FBI had visited Mary's father at the Rock Island Arsenal and knew they were hiding out on a farm—all this had made the decision inevitable. Besides, they had a baby now, and it was getting harder to live the way they had been living—unable to work except for cash, unable to leave a paper trail of any kind. Snowbird would soon be old enough for day care and then school, and he wanted to give her that without worry.

The announcement would have been the first Mary had heard of his decision, or the article in the Des Moines Register. Now, here they sat, as Preston Penny outlined the plan. He would call the FBI and then drive Larry to Des Moines where he would surrender to the U.S. Marshal. He would be arraigned, released on his own recognizance and then a trial date would be set. Mary would "wear a dress and bring the baby," the hippies from the farm would stay home and Larry's parents would testify as character witnesses.

The plan unfolded as outlined, and in the late summer of 1972, Larry and Penny drove the long, straight drive to Des Moines, where Larry surrendered to the authorities. The trial and sentencing were both held there, at the federal court house. The two judges in line for that rotation were Judge Hanson, whose son had resisted the draft, and Judge Stuart, a known hawk. When Stuart was called, Penny decided to request a jury trial, hoping that public opinion would offset the judge's politics.

But the jury foreman—a farmer with a buzz cut and wide tie—immediately disliked Larry. When Larry was asked to state his profession to the court and he answered, "subsistence farmer," the foreman rolled his eyes and grunted. There were women on the jury, too. A teacher, Larry would later remember, and a few others, who seemed sympathetic. But he knew that they could never come up with a verdict other than guilty. He admitted to resisting the draft. The reasons were never allowed to be considered. He couldn't argue that the war was not just. He was not allowed to question the morality of a draft that was, by nature, classist and racist.

He could only stand by his actions.

The trial lasted a full day. The prosecuting attorney, Rick Barry, was a brilliant young lawyer who kept Penny off kilter. His only mistake was in a cross-examination of Larry's father. Barry, in a barrage of routine questions, asked him what he did for a living. Larry's father answered, "I work for the Veteran's Administration." Barry quickly changed the subject.

But Barry recovered when he rested the state's case by asking Larry the lose-lose question that was asked at each draft evasion trial: if you had it to do over again, would you make the same decision? If you answered no, you were free, pending your induction into the armed services. If you answered yes, you could receive a sentence of up to five years in federal prison.

Larry answered yes.

After the trial they all went to dinner at a dark cocktail lounge in Des Moines that smelled of stale cigarettes and sirloin. Then, in just three hours, they were called and told that the jury was back from deliberations. Larry had been found guilty.

The sentencing, which was left up to Judge Stuart, was what would be crucial. Larry could be released, he could get alternative service or he could go to jail. He had known a couple of friends who had been sent to prison as late as 1971, for resisting the draft. Some of them had served a whole year in federal prison and then an alternative duty sentence on top of that when they were released. Larry was fully prepared to face the same.

Mary wore a wool plaid, fitted skirt she had found at Goodwill and a pair of brown patent leather pumps she had worn to the Notre Dame homecoming dance her freshmen year of college, a lifetime ago. But she spent most of the sentencing in the long hallway outside the courtrooms, because Snowbird would not stop screaming.

Before Judge Stuart announced the sentence, Penny had a chance to speak for Larry. He argued passionately that Larry was a pacifist, "violently opposed to war." Larry cringed. Judge Stuart shook his head and asked Penny to sit down. Then he asked Larry if he would like to speak for himself.

Larry stood. He was twenty-five years old, a father now. His blonde hair was cut short for the trial. He was clean-shaven. His two years spent underground now seemed like ten. "First of all," he told the judge, "I'm not violently opposed to anything."

All he had wanted from the beginning, Larry told him, was the chance to serve an alternative duty sentence. He had asked his local draft board for that opportunity and they had denied it. And that's how the situation had gotten to this point. He had never been given a chance to do anything but resist the draft. He was a resister, not a draft evader. This was a distinction he paid particular attention to. He had never run. He had resisted.

After Larry took his seat, Judge Stuart grumbled a short speech about patriotism and then announced the sentence. Larry would have to serve two years in prison. Or, the judge continued after a short pause, two years of alternative duty.

It was a victory, of sorts. Larry had escaped jail time. It was the early seventies and the country was ready to start forgetting. So he took the alternative duty—five nights a week as a janitor at University Hospital. Penny claimed that if he had gotten another judge he might not have been sentenced to anything. Larry was sure that *if he had turned himself in or been picked up a year earlier, he would have served time. Mary was stunned. She had been certain that he would be let off. They had a lawyer. The draft was over. She had lied on the stand, claiming that the trip to Europe was a honeymoon. Besides, everyone knew now that the war had been a mistake. Everyone knew. Larry, on the other hand, was just relieved for it all to finally be over. And so, in the fall of 1972, in his brand-new scrub suit, he set about the nightly routine that would mark the slow disintegration of the life he and Mary had known.*

We get into Iowa and immediately stop at a rest stop so my mother can call Kitt and Roger, old friends who we'll be staying with while I try to find an apartment. She goes inside to use the phone and I count the rest of the mints. Seven. I can see my mother on the pay phone through the glass doors of the brick rest stop building. She is smiling and motioning with her hands.

My mother hasn't seen Kitt in years, since the last time Kitt came out to Portland to visit. The first thing Kitt said when she got to my mother's house was "Let's switch outfits." She was one of those kinds of friends.

I have lots of memories of Kitt and Roger's farm. Their son Ethan had been one of my best friends and I liked listening to Joan Baez records with him and melting his Star Wars figures in the barrel behind the house. He had the Millennium Falcon, a good dog named Emily and a tire swing, and I watched him grow up in photographs Kitt sent my mother. Now we are running late and my mother is worried because Kitt took the afternoon off from her job as a nurse and we won't be getting in until dark anyway.

My mother comes back out and gets into the passenger seat.

"It's okay," she says. "I told her we were meeting Jessica at six and that we'd be out at eight or nine."

Jessica is my older, blonder cousin. When I was four and she was five, she and my mother and I took the train from Iowa down to Texas to visit my grandparents. I had the window seat and I would spend the long hours trying to understand the meaning of the letters on the billboards that flew past. The only words I could spell were *Chelsea* and *flower*. I spent most of that trip with a marker and wide-ruled notebook writing *Chelsea, flower, Chelsea, flower*—breaking the fervor occasionally to glance up angrily at Jessica as she thumbed through *Green Eggs and Ham* or laughed at a witty line in a comic book.

I have been jealous of her ever since.

She lives in Omaha now and we are meeting her at the little amusement park at City Park because it is one of the places in Iowa City I remember loving. She is bringing along her niece, the daughter her brother had when he was fifteen, who we've never met.

"Promise me," Snowbird's mother tells her one day when she is nine, "that you won't get married or have kids until you are twenty-five."

"Okay," says Snowbird, not looking up. She is used to promising.

"I mean it," her mother says.

"Okay," says Snowbird, and she puts down her doll and the Q-tips and bubble bath she has been using to give her a home perm and looks up at her mother. "I promise."

"So," my mother says.

"So."

"Are you going to drive?"

We are still at the rest stop. There is a large man walking a little dog next to a sign that reads: *Keep Dogs on Leash*. The dog is pooping. The man is looking around guiltily to see if anyone is watching.

"In a minute," I say.

"Okay."

The dog finishes its business and the man swoops it up under his arm and carries it back to a mobile home with a Darwin fish on the back. Next to the fish there is a bumper sticker that says *God is Coming, and She is Pissed*. As they walk the man scratches the dog's head with one finger and whispers something to it.

I turn to my mother. "What if we get there, and it turns out that it isn't what I need at all? I'm Depressed Girl in Iowa, instead of Depressed Girl in California? Angst ridden, but corn fed."

I stare at her for a second and then we both start to laugh.

"Look," she says, pointing out the front window at a little girl running with her brother on the grass. "When you were that age you were an Iowan. A farm girl. You were such a grounded little thing—so much a part of the land.

"That was the idea of the farm communes. We all read Wendell Berry and decided to go be 'mad farmers.' We wanted to save you from the havoc and ruin and despair we saw all around us. We wanted you to be free. Like that John Prine song about the peaches."

"What John Prine song?"

"You know, the one with the peaches. We used to listen to

that song all the time. It was our anthem."

"How did it go?"

"Oh, let's see. 'I was young and hungry, about to leave that place, when just as I was leaving she looked me in the face. I said you must know the answer, she said, no but I'll give it a try, and to this very day we've been living our way and here is the reason why:'

"Here comes the chorus." She starts to sing, slow and sweetly. "'Blew up our TV. Threw away the paper. Went out to the country. Built us a home. Had a lot of children. Fed 'em all on peaches. They all found Jesus, on their own.'"

I can't remember the last time I heard her sing. "I can't believe you remember all that."

"It was a good song."

She is still humming the chorus when I start the car and pull back onto the freeway.

After a minute, I turn to her. "I'm glad you're coming with me, Mom. To Iowa City."

She smiles. "Me, too." She gestures out the window. "Just look at this place." On either side of the freeway are acres of countryside. Red elms. Cottonwoods. Farmland. White farm-houses and red barns set off by rolling hills of crops and pas-ture. "I don't know why I left."

At that moment I notice how different the light is here. It's not the bright white of the Northwest or the smog-filtered yellow of Southern California. It's open and blue. Exactly as I remember it.

I glance over at my mother. She looks beautiful to me. Her hair falls below her shoulders, as long as it has been since she first cut it, right before we left the farm. She is wearing black capri pants and a sleeveless black shirt. Creeping above the low neckline of the shirt I can see the scar from where they excised a portion of her shoulder around the melanoma. It has healed well, the flesh is smooth and nearly the color of the rest of her skin, but it is still difficult for me to look at it. It reminds me of my fears—all the possibilities of loss and dread and despair. It reminds me of the unreliability of time.

We drive that last hour to Iowa City in silence, as the sun slides toward the horizon, and I am aware of *all of it*. I am aware of every sound and motion. It is like that feeling right before something happens that changes everything.

We get into town at dusk. It comes up suddenly, after so many hours of corn fields and highway and bad food and imagining. We drive in on Highway 6, past the new Wal-Mart and the new housing development and the lot where the new Red Lobster is going in, and then take a left on Highway 1.

I pop in the Bob Dylan tape because Dylan is who I had always imagined playing as I drove into Iowa City. I listen to his scratchy croon with my head against the window. "I drive up the street to see what I can see in my Cadillac. Good car to drive after a war."

I want to roll down my window and scream and wave my arms. "It's me! I'm back!" But instead I watch the buildings go past and the Iowa River flow by. Then I see a bicycle ramp at the end of an overpass. It winds in a spiral three times, its cement frame graceful and solid, and I remember. I am walking to day care, to Friendship, where I will make animals out of small colored marshmallows and pies out of dirt, and I have to walk up this massive spiraled structure, and it is so beautiful and new and amazing to me that I run as fast as I can to the top just for the pleasure of it.

"Push me on the swing," Snowbird tells her father. They are at City Park in the summertime. She climbs into the swing and holds onto the rusty chains as her father pushes her from behind. Her hands are sticky with pink taffy and her hair is wet and tangled from swimming in the pool and she pumps her feet, pointing her toes the way her father has shown her.

"If you swing high enough," she asks him, "will the swing go all the way around?"

"You would really have to swing hard," he explains, "for that to happen."

"Underdog me," Snowbird tells him. And he does, pushing her from behind and then running underneath the swing. "UNDERDOG!" they both yell as he comes through in front of her.

"Tell me again, about what happens to people who suck their thumbs too long," Snowbird says.

"Their teeth grow out long like a walrus's."

"And what happens to people who do somersaults off the couch?"

"Their shoulders grow big and round like a football player's."

"And what happens when you eat orange seeds?"

"An orange tree grows in your stomach and out your ears."

Snowbird grins and grips the rusty chains tighter. "Push me higher," she tells him.

And he does.

~

We get to City Park and the smell is warm and sweet, like grass. My mother pulls into a gravel parking space and when the white dust settles we see Jessica, even blonder than the last time I saw her, holding a wiggling child.

We pull our stiff bodies out of the car to greet her, and my mother hugs her before I do. Jessica introduces us to Kayla, her niece, and to Kayla's mother, who is nineteen, and to Kayla's mother's friend, who is also nineteen. They both have permed hair and are wearing white sneakers and frosted lipstick.

The little amusement park where we are standing is exactly as I remember it, although I find out later that most of it was washed away and replaced after the Big Flood of 1993. There is a merry-go-round, a refreshment stand and a ferris wheel. This was always my favorite ride, because, if you craned hard enough, when you got to the top you could grab a leaf off the lower branches of a big tree. The big tree is dead now, but I ask Jessica and Kayla if they want to ride the ferris wheel, anyway.

We pay fifty cents a person and give our tickets to the operator and he grinds the ride to a halt and lets us on. The seats are small and our weight sends our bench immediately rocking. The operator steadies us and pulls down the metal guardrail, locking it into place with a clang. Then he pulls a big lever and we are off, lifting up above the merry-go-round and the refreshment stand and my old tan Honda Accord. We lift up and over and down again and around and up and Kayla starts to cry when she sees the people below. Jessica makes soft, cooing noises at her and tickles her tummy while I watch the sky and the green trees, thinking about handfuls of shredded leaves stuffed in my pocket and diligently squirreled away.

"Look," Jessica says to Kayla, who is still wailing. "Look. Look." And Kayla and I look down and see our mothers and they are smiling up at us and waving. We wave and shout something back, but they are too far away to hear.

On the last Halloween Snowbird is in Iowa City, she is Autumn. Her mother spends all week sitting on the porch of the brown house, sewing fragile, dry leaves on a cloak she has made out of a white bed sheet. When she is done, Snowbird and her mother march in a parade downtown, but her mother keeps stopping to help the little angel in front of them whose wings keep coming unsnapped.

"You love that little angel more than you love me," Snowbird accuses her mother.

"It's true," her mother tells her. "She is my real daughter. You are just a baby that the gypsies left on my porch."

"I am your real daughter," Snowbird tells her, "because we have the same nose."

Her mother shakes her head no. "I bought our noses at the same store," she explains.

Snowbird thinks about this. "You can't buy noses."

"Yes, that's true," her mother tells her. "But these were used noses."

Snowbird thinks some more. "I know that you're my real mother," she says.

"How do you know?"

"Because you love me."

"Ahh," says her mother.

One night in the summertime, Snowbird is sitting on the top step of the side porch, dangling her feet over the edge and eating a Fig Newton, when she thinks she sees the Snowqueen's face in the moon, just as she'd promised. She squints, the way she's been practicing, but the vision goes away.

She imagines that the Snowqueen is there, though, living in the moon. She is tall and pale, with long, white-and-silver robes and thin wrists. Her eyes are bright, and her pockets are full of magic moon dust.

After the ferris wheel ride, my mother and I get back into my car and Jessica, Kayla, Kayla's mother and Kayla's mother's friend get back into Jessica's car and we lead the way downtown and park in a parking garage. We spend a half-hour walking around looking for a restaurant and then give up and go to a pizza place where my mother and I order a pizza with basil and goat cheese. The others order spaghetti.

It takes a long time for dinner to come so Jessica tells us about how she is up for this job doing public relations for the symphony and how she is seeing this wonderful man and how the University of Iowa is asking her—practically begging her—to attend their law school next year.

I choke on a piece of bread and almost die, but no one notices.

Snowbird and her father are at City Park. They have been swimming and then to the swings and now, on their way back to the little red Triumph, they pass a volleyball game.

The net is strung up between two trees and there are two teams of men on either side scurrying to hit the ball over it. One of the men is bald and has only one leg.

Snowbird's father sees her staring.

"Wow," he says, so she can hear. "That man is a really good volleyball player."

"What do you think, Chelsea?" I hear Jessica ask me.

"What?" I am eating a piece of pizza and staring out the window at a girl walking a big dog on a leash.

Jessica sighs. "About what your mother said. About you being a voyager into the soul." I can tell she is amused.

"A psychonaut," I say.

"What?"

"A psychonaut," I repeat. "It's from *The Tibetan Book of the Dead*."

"The what?"

"Never mind," I say.

Snowbird's first words are in French.

"*La lune!*" she cries in her mother's arms one night, pointing at the moon. "*La luuunnnee. La lune. La luuunnee!*" Her mother has been teaching her this other language, pointing at the window and saying, "*la fenêtre*," and pointing at the toy purple Volkswagen bug and saying, "*l'auto*."

"*La lune!*" Snowbird cries to her father and Donnie and Shelley and Curt and Cunningham and Elliott. "*La lune!*" None of them speak a word of French, but they all seem to understand.

"Are you listening to me?" Jessica's voice has an edge.

"Yes," I say, pulling my gaze back into the restaurant.

Kayla is decorating the table with noodles and her mother and her mother's friend are reapplying their frosted lipstick. My mother and Jessica are staring at me.

"You're really being weird," Jessica says.

I want to flee from the table and run and see how tall the tree is that we planted in front of my old brown house; I want to try to find Donnie and I want to see a lightning bug. Instead I say: "I'm just distracted. It's been a long drive."

The check comes and my mother buys everyone dinner. Then we all walk back to the parking garage. My mother tells Jessica how much we've enjoyed the visit and tells Kayla and Kayla's mother and Kayla's mother's friend how nice it was to meet them.

Then we hug and say good-bye and Jessica tells me that I ought to drive to Omaha and visit her some weekend. I tell her I won't be driving anywhere for a while and get into the car.

Jessica and the others follow us out of the parking garage in Jessica's shiny white Honda. After we take a left she takes a right and disappears around a corner.

We head back out on Highway 1 to Kitt and Roger's farm. It is dark but hot enough that we have the windows open and the wind blows my hair across my face. There are no sounds of traffic here. No sirens. No car alarms. Only a lot of very quiet cows.

And so I'm in Iowa. Just like that. It's a little unsettling when you've thought about something your whole life, and then suddenly find yourself doing it. Sort of like wanting to be an astronaut since you were a kid—you study physics, you get accepted by NASA, you.train and then one day you find yourself staring at the earth from a rocket window. "Strange," you think to yourself. "I never thought it would be quite so blue." Or round. Or big. Or small. Not because it isn't what you wanted it to be, but because you can't imagine that you are actually there. Maybe you've always thought of life as that railroad track from your favorite Allen Ginsberg poem—rusty and surrounded by yellow flowers, heading straight past into the distance. And now here you are, and it turns out that the tracks don't go straight ahead at all, but rather in a circle that gets tighter and tighter, pulling you closer in. To where?

"Why are you a Buddhist?" I ask. We are still a few minutes from Kitt and Roger's farm.

My mother leans closer to the steering wheel so she can see better into the dark countryside. "A student of Buddhism," she corrects me. "I am a student of Buddhism because it gives me pleasure."

"Is that why you meditate?"

"For the pleasure of it? I guess so. When I used to meditate years ago, I hated it. I couldn't wait until it was over. Now I look forward to it. The pleasure is in the giving over of one's self to the idea of it."

"The idea of meditation?"

"The idea of stillness." She looks at me. "You should try it."

"I have tried it. My legs get stiff."

"Then you haven't given yourself over to the idea yet."

"The idea of stillness," I say.

"The idea of Buddhism."

"Can't I be a Buddhist simply because I am your daughter? The way that you were a Catholic because your parents were Catholic?"

"No." My mother shakes her head. "Remember when we were in that store and you saw the little amber Buddha charm and you wanted to buy it and wear it on a necklace?"

"Yeah."

"Buddhists don't wear little amber Buddha charms around their necks. It would be considered missing the point."

"Ah," I counter. "But Catholics wear crosses."

"Exactly," my mother says.

We pull up to Kitt and Roger's around nine and park the car next to the barn they are rebuilding. My mother honks the horn and Kitt, Roger and Ethan come running out of the house to greet us.

Kitt's hair is layered and it bobs up and down as she hugs my mother. Roger stands off to the side, playing with his beard. Ethan smiles at me shyly.

"Hey," he says.

"Hey," I say.

We go inside past the old chicken coop and the tree where Ethan's tire swing used to be and Kitt takes us on a tour of the house and shows us all the remodeling she's done. It looks exactly the same to me.

Then we go into the kitchen and sit around the kitchen table talking about nothing until my mother and I are yawning between words and Kitt offers to show us where we'll be sleeping.

"Come with me," she says, and we get our overnight bags from the car and get into Kitt's car and she drives us to the other side of their pond to the little guesthouse.

Once Kitt finally leaves, my mother and I crawl into the big double bed. The whirl of the electric fan is so loud even the sounds of the frogs melt away. I am back in Iowa, I think to myself. Strange.

Snowbird's mother is sleeping on the couch in the white house. Snowbird watches her breathe through her nose and the tiny movements her eyes make under her eyelids. She watches her chest move up and down and the way her hair is tangled across her face and then she climbs onto the couch and stretches out on top of her mother's body. Her mother wakes up under the weight and looks at Snowbird and sighs. She looks at her watch and stretches her arms behind her head and then they both lie quietly for a long time.

Snowbird cuddles against her neck so she is right next to her ear. "Who is God?" she whispers.

Her mother doesn't move. "Catholics believe that God is everybody's father," she says.

"Are we Catholic?"

"No."

"Are Grandma and Grandpa?"

"Yes."

"Is my dad?"

"No."

Snowbird considers this. "Who is God, really?"

"I can't tell you that," her mother says. "Because different people believe different things. You have to decide for yourself who you think God is."

"But who do you think God is?"

Her mother is quiet for a minute. "I don't believe in God," she says.

Snowbird cuddles against her soft smell and plays with the skin on her mother's cheek. "Oh," she says, pushing the flesh in with her finger and watching it bounce back out.

I n the back seat of my car, underneath my guitar, my albums and my clothes, are two photo albums. They are filled with pictures of the three farms we lived on, mostly taken by visiting family members. After my mom got sick, I spent a summer sorting through my mother's closetful of old photographs, putting the albums together. It seemed important to me to separate the farm pictures from the others—as if piecing them all together would help me see a larger picture. There are photographs of Kitt, her hair bouncy even then, and Ethan and me cavorting naked in the garden. There is one of Colleen asleep on the couch, and a few of Curt and Shelley. There are many of my mom and dad and me. But there are only two of Donnie. In two whole photo albums I have only two pictures to remember him by.

On the way to Iowa I asked my mother why he was so often omitted. She explained how Donnie would usually leave to make room when anyone came to visit and that was why he was never in any of the photos taken by visitors. Other than that, the only camera at the farm was his, and the only pictures he took were of me.

Snowbird has known Donnie her whole life. She likes the story about how he came to the farm—how he was living with his two crazy aunts and one of them sent him to check up on the hippies who were renting one of her houses. He came by on a Saturday and moved in a few months later.

Later, when Snowbird and her mother move to the apartment in his blue house in town, he gives her peanut rolls and lets her come over and sit with him when he watches "The Streets of San Francisco" on TV.

"Hello, hello," he always says when he sees her, and then he tells her stories about his Aunt Florence's two hundred dogs and how his Aunt Cora hasn't walked since her feet turned blue.

Sometimes, when he isn't telling stories about his aunts, they will sit in his big red chair and he will read her *Rootabaga Stories*. "How They Bring Back the Village of Cream Puffs When the Wind Blows It Away" is Snowbird's favorite because it is about a little girl just like her who goes to visit her uncles in the Village of Liver-and-Onions. The uncles gather round asking her silly questions, like how she got the two freckles on her chin, and the little girl, who likes her uncles very much, tells them.

"The freckles are put on," answered Wing Tip the Spick. "When a girl goes away from the Village of Cream Puffs her mother puts on two freckles, on the chin. Each freckle must be the same as a little

burnt cream puff kept in the oven too long. After the two freckles looking like two little burnt cream puffs are put on her chin, they remind the girl every morning when she combs her hair and looks in the looking glass. They remind her where she came from and she mustn't stay away too long."

Donnie reads this story the most, because he knows it is Snowbird's favorite, but the one he loves is "The Two Sky-scrapers who Decided to Have a Child." When he reads it he gives the Skyscrapers high squeaky voices.

And they decided when their child came it should be a free child.

"It must be a free child," they said to each other. "It must not be a child standing still all its life on a street corner. Yes, if we have a child she must be free to run across the prairie, to the mountains, to the sea. Yes, it must be a free child."

One day when Snowbird is over in Donnie's side of the blue house, she cuts her thumb slicing ham with a knife. The red blood runs in long drips from the cut and winds around her wrist.

"Donnie," she says, holding out her thumb toward him. "Donnie, look."

He is sitting in the red chair, watching television, and it is a few seconds before he glances up. When he does he jumps up and runs to her side, wrapping her hand in a blue dishtowel and then holding it in both of his.

"I'm sorry," he keeps saying over and over again. "I'm sorry."

Snowbird can feel the pulse of his fingers through the towel. She does not say anything and they stay like that, per-fectly still, until the bleeding stops.

∽

The day before Snowbird leaves Iowa City, she and Donnie walk downtown. She likes to walk with Donnie because he stoops over a bit to one side so that they can hold hands. They go to Baskin-Robbins, because this is what Snowbird wants, and Donnie buys her a strawberry ice cream cone and an Orange Crush and then they go to a little gift store and Donnie buys her two small stuffed animals she sees in the window.

Donnie holds up the little pink bunny rabbit. "This will be you," he says, and he holds up the little yellow chicken. "And this will be me." He hands them to Snowbird who pins them both to her belly with one arm, because she is still holding the can of Orange Crush with the other. "So whenever they're together, we'll be a little bit together too."

"What should we name them?" Snowbird asks.

"What about something from *Rootabaga Stories?*"

Snowbird thinks about this. "Skyscraper isn't a very good name for a rabbit," she says.

"No," says Donnie. "I guess not."

They think some more. "What about Wing Tip the Spick?" Donnie suggests.

"That's a pretty long name," Snowbirds says after she has considered it.

Donnie scratches his chin. "I know," he says after a pause. "How about Bunny and Chick?"

Snowbird smiles. "I like those names," she says, and repeats them out loud to make sure they sound as good when she says them. She looks down at Bunny and Chick to see what they think. They are both smiling. "I like those names," she says again. And she kisses them each on the forehead and then has Donnie kiss them each on the forehead to make it official.

That night, when he says good-bye, Donnie leans his forehead against hers and thanks her for all the times she rubbed his temples and sang songs. She whispers in his ear that she loves him the most, except for her mother and father, out of all the grown-ups she knows.

He reaches inside his jacket and pulls out a package wrapped in newspaper funnies. She opens it—it is his hard-back copy of *James and the Giant Peach*, his favorite book.

She will have it, and the two stuffed animals, for her whole childhood.

He calls every couple of years after that, talking for as long he can before the quarters run out. Always in the middle of the night. Always from a bar. Always drunk.

When Snowbird is fourteen, he stops calling.

I wake up thinking of Donnie and look for my mother, but she has already gone. A note in the kitchen says that she has walked over to the main house and to follow the trail.

I get dressed and go outside. Although it is barely nine o'clock, the air already is heavy with heat. The trail starts at the base of the cabin, leads around the little pond and then carves into a huge, green meadow. The wild grass is taller than I am and I can hear turkeys running out of sight as I approach. It is muddy. Iowa mud. Mud that sucks your feet into the earth as you walk. I remember something about lying by the pond with Ethan, picking ticks off the dogs—how we would pull apart their fur, clump by clump, searching, and then tug the ticks off with our fingers and watch them scurry into the mud.

I get to the top of a hill where the trail splits in two directions and realize that I have no idea which way to go. I choose a path and it bends around another little pond and then up a hill and soon I see Kitt and Roger's house. Their black dog sees me and bounds over from his spot on the porch.

~

I can smell the coffee as soon as I walk inside and I find Kitt and Roger bent over a one-cup coffee maker in the kitchen, trying to keep up with my mother, who is sitting at the kitchen table with her just-emptied mug.

"Good morning," they all say brightly.

"Good morning," I say. I take the chair across from my mother, fold my arms on the table and lean forward. "Today I want to try to find Donnie."

"Donnie?" Kitt asks. "I haven't seen him in years."

My mother points behind me at a little table where a phone book is sitting. "Go to it," she says.

I reach back and get the phone book, which is divided by community, and I look through every section and don't see his name.

"Now what?" I ask.

Kitt comes to the table and pours my mother another cup of coffee and my mother takes two big sips. "What about his brother?" Kitt asks.

My mother takes another sip from her mug and Kitt goes back to the coffee maker.

Then my mother leafs through the phone book, tracing the names with her finger. After a minute her finger stops. "Ah ha," she says.

"Ah ha?"

My mother rotates the phone book so I can see where her finger is pointing. She has found Donnie's brother. "So call him," I say. She gives me the number and I dial it for her and then pull the phone receiver to her so she doesn't have to get up.

"Is this Paul?" I hear her ask. "This is Mary Cain, Donnie's friend. My daughter and I are back in town and we wanted to get in touch with him." I can tell from my mother's reaction that Paul isn't much help and they make small talk for a few minutes and then she hands me the phone. I hang it back in its cradle. "Well?"

"They haven't talked in ten years," she says. "The last Paul heard, Donnie was still living in the blue house on Johnson Street."

"So let's try there."

"Didn't your dad try Johnson Street when he looked for Donnie the last time he was in town?"

"I don't know," I sigh. "Come on, it'll be great to see the place."

"Okay, we'll do it," my mom says as Kitt appears with another cup of coffee.

I hold up my empty mug toward Kitt. "That," I tell my mother, "is my cup."

"Tell me about Donnie's aunts," I ask my mother. We are speeding back down Highway 6 toward town and my mother has just announced that we are down to the last five mints.

"I knew Florence better than Cora," she says, "since we had to help her with the dogs."

"Like getting the food?" I ask, already knowing the answer.

"Yeah," my mother says. "We'd get in the truck and head into Coralville to the bakery. We would fill the whole back of the truck with stale bread and then we'd go to the butcher and he would give us all the animal parts no one would buy and then we'd haul the whole load to Florence's."

"And she'd give it to the dogs?"

"She'd boil the meat in a huge pot of water and pour it over the bread until it was all soft mush and she'd feed that to the dogs."

"And they were able to live on that?"

"They were as crazy as she was."

"Wasn't anyone concerned about her—this little old crazy woman living on a farm with two hundred crazy dogs?"

"I don't know," my mother says. "Back then they just kind of left crazy people alone. The place was filthy, though. Florence lived in the kitchen and the rest of the house was filled with dog feces. Your dad used to keep a pair of overalls in the barn especially for going over there. And the stench was incredible."

"But you still kept going over when she'd call."

"After a while, it started to seem almost normal, part of the routine. The phone would ring at four in the morning and it would be Florence screaming 'Help! They're killing me!' And Larry would go out in the barn and pull on the overalls and then go over and break up whatever dogs happened to be fighting that night."

"And Donnie grew up around this?"

"He grew up with Cora, but she was as nuts as Florence."

"She was the one with the blue feet," I say, remembering.

"Yeah. She had diabetes and she stayed in her bed in her living room all day long, yelling so loud the horses would paw the ground in her barn."

"Where were Donnie's parents?"

"I don't know what happened to his mother," my mother says. "But I remember him saying that his dad was a drunk."

"Did Donnie drink back then? I mean, did he drink too much, back at the farm?"

"No more than the rest of us. He seemed really good. He was so happy to get away from Cora and so good with you. It didn't get bad really until we all moved."

We are quiet for a minute and I realize for the first time how very humid it is in the summertime in Iowa. "He's dead," I say. "Isn't he?"

"Get away from that tree trunk, you stupid boy!" Aunt Spiker yelled. "The slightest shake and I'm sure it'll fall off! It must weigh twenty or thirty pounds at least!"

The branch that the peach was growing upon was beginning to bend over further and further because of the weight.

"Stand back!" Aunt Sponge shouted. "It's coming down! The branch is going to break!"

But the branch didn't break. It simply bent over more and more as the peach got heavier and heavier.

My mother pulls the car to the curb in front of Donnie's old house on Johnson Street and says, "Here it is."

It takes me a minute to recognize the place because it isn't blue anymore. But once my eyes adjust to the new white color, I can see it as it was: the porch swing to the right of the porch, the two front doors, side by side, one leading to Donnie's apartment, one to ours.

The grass is overgrown and weedy, and I remember how my mother tilled the strip of lawn between the sidewalk and street and planted a vegetable garden and how the city made her plow it under.

We are still sitting in the car and my mother says: "When I told you we were going to move into town, your only condition was that we move into a blue house. I told Donnie that and the two of us and some other friends spent a weekend that summer painting his place 'dusty azure.' It was a terrible color, but you loved it."

"I don't remember that," I say.

We sit in the car a few more minutes, looking at the house. The window of Donnie's old apartment is cracked and taped with duct tape. "He doesn't live here anymore," my mother says. "He would never let it get this bad."

"Let's try, anyway," I say, and we get out of the car and walk up to the porch I haven't stood on since I was six years old.

My mother knocks and a pudgy man in his early twenties comes to the door with a beer in his hand and a T-shirt that says *Just Visiting This Planet.*

My mother asks him if he knows anyone named Donnie and he says no, that the place is now owned by some rental company.

"Let's go," I say quietly before she asks if we can come in and look around. I don't want to see it like this. I don't want to see it without Donnie.

We drive back in silence and when we arrive we tell Kitt about our bad luck. "What about that guy," she says, "that guy he used to know?"

"That guy?" I ask.

"You know," she says pointing at my mother. "That guy who sold stoves, the one who always wore that silly knife on his belt."

"Oh," my mother says. "Right. His friend, Jerry."

"Call him," I say. Flipping the phone book on the table.

"Call him," says Kitt.

"I don't want to call him," my mother says. "You call him." She pushes the phonebook toward Kitt and she finds the number and picks up the phone and dials.

"Hello, Jerry? This is Kitt Boldt. Mary Cain is in town with her daughter and they're trying to find Donnie—"

After a few minutes she hangs up the phone and bobs her hair in defeat. "He hasn't seen him in years."

"I don't know what else to do," my mother says.

We all sit for a minute, staring at each other. "What about finding Cora or Florence?" Kitt asks.

"They both died years ago," I explain. "My dad went out to see them the last time he was here. The houses were condemned."

"We tried," my mother says.

"Yes," Kitt says.

"Yes," I say.

"We tried," my mother says again.

W e decide not to go back into town until dinner and instead spend the rest of the afternoon at Kitt's, who has somehow managed to take another day off from the hospital. She and my mother go down to the pond for a swim and I sit on the front porch in the sun, reading. I have just finished a chapter and am waving a persistent swarm of bugs away when I spot another farmhouse on the next hill. It is white and surrounded by trees and a few outbuildings.

"Looks about the same, doesn't it?" my mother asks, coming back early from her swim to escape the bugs.

I squint, but can't bring the farmhouse any closer. "That's the farm?" I ask.

"Yeah," my mother says.

"I didn't know it was so close."

"Sure," my mother says. "That's how we met Kitt and Roger. I brought them over some beer the day we moved in."

"Do Kitt and Roger know who lives there?"

"Some French woman who bakes bread and teaches at the university."

I look at the farm, and then back at my mother. "It looks beautiful from here."

That night Kitt and Roger, Ethan, my mother and I decide to go into town to a bar called The Sanctuary for dinner. On the way Roger takes us by the old brown house my mother and I used to live in on Gilbert Street. It is encased in gray vinyl siding now and the side yard has been paved to allow for off-street parking. But the tree we planted is still there, saved from the cement truck by a few feet of grass. It is as tall as the house now, and I am amazed by its growth until I remember that it has been eighteen years since we planted it.

We find a place to park downtown and the five of us walk around so my mother and I can see how things have changed. The area has been closed off to cars and made into a pedestrian mall. Still I recognize buildings: the theater where I saw *Star Wars* with my dad, and MacBride Hall with its natural history museum filled with rows and rows of stuffed dead birds.

We are headed down Dubuque Street when I see a bookstore that I used to love called Prairie Lights and I convince the others to come in with me to look around. We are inside only a few minutes before they abandon me for the new coffee bar upstairs.

It is loud and I am in the corner looking at the journals.

"Hey," Kitt says, appearing at my side, grinning. "I want to show you something."

"Okay," I say slowly. And I let her lead me toward the cafe.

We go up the four stairs and work our way between the white tables toward my mother and Roger and Ethan who are talking to two strangers. My mother is flushed and laughing.

We get closer and one of the strangers, a man with short, brown hair and tortoise shell-rimmed glasses, looks up at me. Smiles. His eyes are clear and bright and his clothes are pressed. I look at Kitt, who is still grinning, and then back at the stranger. My arms feel light.

"Donnie?" I ask.

"Hello, hello," he says, extending his hand.

I feel, in that second, as if I have just learned something terribly important but I don't know what yet. *"It's just the porch light."*

"Donnie?" I say again.

He nods. His eyes wet, his whole body shaking just a little. He opens up his arms and I hug him and I have never been more glad not to live in Southern California.

"I'm taller," I say, although I am having trouble talking.

He nods. Grins. Then he introduces me to the woman sitting at his table, with whom he has lived for the past nine years. They raised her daughter, he tells me, Mariah. And I say that I would like very much to meet her.

I pull out a chair and join them at the table. I know that if I say another word I will fall apart and Donnie just keeps nodding. My mother, who had fallen apart before I'd even gotten there, suggests that the three of us get together tomorrow morning and we agree to meet at another coffee place Donn knows.

As we get up to leave to make our dinner reservation The Sanctuary I hear my mother say to Donnie, "So, yc stopped drinking."

"Bare minimum," I hear him answer back. "Bare mum."

I don't hear a thing anybody says at dinner.

145

~

We meet Donnie at seven the next morning on the front porch of The Cottage, a coffee place only a few blocks away from Prairie Lights. He is sitting at a table outside, combed and ironed like a kid on his way to a party.

He stands up when he sees us and gives us both hugs.

"I'm sorry I was so in shock last night," he says, sitting down. "You caught me by surprise."

"You caught us by surprise, too," I tell him. But I don't tell him why.

"The last time I saw you," he says to me, "you were this tall." He holds out his hand palm down about four feet above the porch and grins.

My mother gets up and goes inside to buy us coffee, leaving Donnie and me outside, staring at each other.

I wonder if I would have recognized him if I had passed him on the street. He looks healthy. His face has color and he isn't as thin as I remember. I find myself thinking that with his short hair and preppie clothes, he looks like a sitcom dad, or maybe an architect.

"What do you do now?" I ask.

"Oh, stuff and things," he says, "stuff and things. I've been painting a bit this summer." He reaches into his wallet and fishes out a blue business card and hands it to me. It has a drawing of a paintbrush above his name and another man's. "We've been doing it every summer for the past eight years. It's good money and fun when you get a good job. In the winter I work out at NCS, grading tests." And I remember how surprised I was when my GRE scores arrived postmarked Iowa City.

My mother reappears with coffee and croissants for us both and sits down.

"What do you hear about the others?" he asks her.

"Not a lot," she says. "We don't keep in touch with anyone. Last I heard Elliott was married and had a new baby. They

146

live in Oregon. Krista, of course, died a few years ago. You heard about that?" He nods. "Cunningham has some sort of job in the computer department at Madison. Curt and Shelley live in Kansas with their kids. And Bob and Fern were in Key West for a while, but they moved years ago. Larry still lives in Florida. He tried to find you a few years ago."

"Oh?" says Donnie.

My mother lets it go. "Do you keep in touch with anyone?"

"Oh, no," says Donnie. "No. I hear that Patty went to beauty school, though. She took care of Richard for a while, after his wife left him and took the five boys, and he lost the family farm. But now she has some sort of fancy hair salon in D.C. And Tracy's back in town. She works down the street at a vintage clothing store called Ragstock. She cut her hair. You'd never recognize her."

My mother leans forward over the table. "Can you believe it's been twenty years?" she asks.

Donnie smiles and shakes his head. He looks at me. "And now you've come back. After all this time."

"Yeah," I say, though it doesn't seem that long ago to me.

"You know," my mothers says, suddenly, "Chelsea wanted to go out and take a look at the farms, but I have to fly back to Portland tomorrow and I don't think we'll have time. Maybe the two of you could go."

I look at Donnie. "Sure," he says. "I'd like that."

And so he is alive. He is sitting across from me at a table in Iowa City after we had all pretty much let him go. Not because we didn't want to believe he wasn't still around—that his life could not have possibly continued after we had all left—but because it seemed so plausible, so realistic. He had been a drunk, after all. And yet, while we were all silently agreeing that he had died, he was, in fact, in love, raising a child, designing blue business cards with paintbrushes on them and drinking coffee in bookstores.

This is the lesson, says a voice in my head. *This is what you're supposed to understand.* We thought that when we left the farm, that it was over, that without us there it ceased to exist. But experiences don't die, they live with you. Like Donnie, we had accepted the farm as a memory, while silently believing that its influences were long past. But I still remember the sound those boots made on my dad's porch. And I still remember the smell of the dirt from that day we buried Linda. And I still know the glow of a lightning bug. I still live here. Somehow this is still my place, just as it is still a part of all of us.

"You used to give me peanut rolls," I say to Donnie. "Remember?"

He smiles. "I used to buy them twelve to a package so I'd always have a few around whenever you'd come over."

"And read to me."

"Yes. And sometimes you would come over and rub my temples. I used to love that."

"Yes. Or sometimes we would walk downtown and you would buy me ice cream."

"Yes," he says. "I remember."

We talk for a little while longer, though mostly we all just sit and grin at each other, until my mother announces that it is time to go apartment hunting. She and Donnie exchange addresses and promise to keep in touch and I tuck his blue business card in my wallet and promise to call him when I get settled so we can go on a tour of the old houses, though somehow it doesn't seem as important anymore to see the actual physical places.

My mother and I spend the afternoon going through the newspapers and making appointments to see apartments and then I take the first one I get in to see—an overpriced, tiny studio that hasn't been cleaned in years. Because I am a Californian, I decide it is a great deal.

The new apartment is in a big, white house on Burlington Street, just a few blocks from Donnie's old blue house and College Park where my dad taught me how to throw a frisbee. After I sign the lease I suggest that we go to the park.

My mother agrees, so we drive the few blocks and find a place to stretch out on the grass and talk.

It is hot the way it can only be hot in the summertime in Iowa and the park is littered with the bodies of sunbathers, some of whom look like they haven't moved since the last time I was here. It is bright so we lie on our backs with our arms over our eyes to shield them from the sun.

"Remember the Snowqueen?" I ask after we have been lying there for a minute.

"Of course," my mother says.

"She never came after we left Iowa."

"No," my mother says, "I guess she didn't."

"Why do you think that is?"

"Well, you were getting older."

"I used to think it was because she didn't know where to find me. That she had lost track of me after everyone had stopped calling me Snowbird."

"The Snowqueen doesn't lose track of people," my mother says.

"But I missed her."

"She was always right there in the moon if you really needed her. And when you were very happy or very sad, she was right there, right up in the sky. You just weren't squinting hard enough to see her. Besides, if you needed her, all you had to do was ask."

"Yes," I say, lifting my arm off my face and rolling over on my side. "But then you would have known that I knew she was you."

"I knew you knew. You were always watching me with those little blue eyes. Always listening." She smiles. "My little dharma girl."

Back at Kitt and Roger's farm that night, Roger makes pizza and I stand on the back porch and watch a hundred lightning bugs fly just beyond my fingers.

The drive from Iowa City to Chicago has flown by. But it takes my mother and me twenty minutes to find our way from the parking lot into the terminal at O'Hare International

Airport. We park in the wrong lot and then miss the tunnel that leads underground into the main building. After getting lost in a parking garage we are trying to take a shortcut through, we finally ask someone for directions and make it inside.

"I wish I could stay longer," my mother says, standing at her gate as the other passengers board.

"Me too," I say. Then I add: "I'm really glad you came with me."

"Well, I had to come with you," she says. "I'm your mother."

I give her a long hug. "Come back and visit me."

"Yes."

"Promise?"

"Yes."

"And you'll take care of yourself—your health, I mean."

"Yes."

I let her go and she steps back. "Love you," she says.

"I love you too."

Then she starts down the ramp, but turns back after a few steps.

"Oh," she calls back. "I left you the mints. They're in the glove compartment."

"Are there any left?"

"A couple," she says. "But remember, you can always reuse the tin."

When I get back to Iowa City, I head straight to my new apartment and start to unpack my car, carrying it all, box by box, up to the second floor. My new neighbor comes out and asks if I need any help, but I tell him no, because all of a sudden it seems important to do it completely on my own.

The next morning, after all the boxes are stacked in neat columns on my floor, I walk back down to College Park and call my father on the pay phone.

"Dad," I say when he picks up the phone. "I need to ask

you something." He is sitting in the hammock strung up between two palm trees outside his house in Florida and I can
actually hear birds chirping in the background.

"Yeah?" he asks.

"Where did the name Snowbird come from?"

He pauses. "Isn't it because you were born in that blizzard?"

"No," I say. "No. Think, Dad. I really want to know."

He is quiet for a minute, then he starts to laugh. "Oh," he
says. "I remember now. Oh God."

"What?"

"It's from—it's from an Anne Murray song."

"What?"

"You know, 'little snowbird returning from the cold.'"

"It's from an *Anne Murray* song?"

"Please don't tell anyone. I swear I never owned an Anne
Murray album. I must have heard it on the radio."

"It's from an *Anne Murray* song?"

He's really laughing now.

"Jesus," he says, gasping. "I haven't thought of that in
years."

25

The trip journal that my mother and I kept on our journey is actually a spiral notebook that we bought in a grocery store somewhere in Idaho. It is filled with strange little drawings of jackalopes, portraits of each other and anything that either of us said that the other thought was funny enough to write down.

After I have unpacked a little, and my new futon and two new chairs from Goodwill have made my apartment look somewhat livable, I bring up the notebook from my car.

Looking through it, our trip seems like one of my Iowa photo albums, filled with snapshots that, if put in the right order, somehow tell a story. There are two drawings I like the best. One is the picture my mother drew of the Iowa corn goddess. The drawing looks oddly familiar to me the first few times I look at it. Then I realize that it is because the corn goddess looks very much how I imagined the Snowqueen. They were one and the same. It is the only page I tear out of the journal. I tack it up over my desk on the frame of a window that looks out over an old cottonwood tree.

My other favorite is a portrait my mother drew of me with a thin-tipped gray marker. It is a profile of me behind the wheel, wearing sunglasses, my hair pulled back at the base of my neck. I have my eyes on the road, concentrating on driving, my jaw locked in a study in determination. I am driving back to Iowa.

I look at both of those drawings a lot the first few weeks, in between long walks and remembering.

I have been in Iowa City for almost three weeks when I finally go into Ragstock. There I watch a tall, thin woman with short blonde hair reach into a bin of clothes, pull out a piece of clothing, shake it and hang it on a rack. She is wearing tight, black stretch pants, high heels and a bright red sweater. Her face is stern as she goes about her project: stoop, reach, pull, shake, hang. I watch her a little longer, halfheartedly flipping through layers of short black dresses as I try to work up the courage to introduce myself.

I am just about to approach her when she turns on her heels and heads off to a back room. I think I have missed my chance and am starting to leave when she reappears with another armload of clothes. Before I can think better of it I find myself talking to her.

"Um," I stammer. "You're Tracy, right?"

She drops the armload of clothes in the bin. "Teresa."

Teresa. But of course it is too late now, and I have no choice but to plunge ahead. "Uh, I think you knew my mother." Her face is blank, stern. I continue: "Mary Cain?"

She looks at me, holding my gaze, and then suddenly her

whole face seems to open up and she takes a step back, almost knocking over the rack she has been filling. "Oh, my God," she says. "I used to hold you when you were a tiny baby. Oh, my God."

It is Tracy. "I'm sorry I had your name wrong," I say. "I must have misunderstood."

"No, no," she says. "Teresa's not my real name. I got tired of Tracy, you know? So I changed my name to Teresa when I left Iowa to go to art school. Lived in Chicago and Paris and New Mexico. Then a few years ago I had, like, a major nervous breakdown and realized that the only time I'd ever been happy was here." She waves her arms around the store. "So I came back. Got this job. It isn't much but, hell, I'm sane. It's funny, but when I saw you wandering around, you reminded me of your mother. Not just the way you look, but the way you were looking. Like you were really someplace else."

I like her, though I'm not sure why. "Hey," she says, "whatever happened to that cute father of yours?" So I tell her about my parents—about my father and how much I missed him growing up, and about my mother and how even though it's been two years since the melanoma I'm still terrified that she might die. I tell her about seeing Donnie and how when I saw him I loved him exactly as much as when I was six years old. I tell her what I know about Curt and Shelley and Elliott and the others. And I tell her about how I've always wanted to come back to Iowa.

"Yeah," she says. "It's like some sort of spell, isn't it?"

"Yes," I say. "Yes, exactly."

The woman at the counter smiles at us and Tracy says, "Hey, you want to know how old I am? I used to live on a commune with her mother. I used to hold her when she was a baby." Tracy introduces the woman to me. Then she turns to the woman and sweeps her arm through the air in a grand gesture of introduction:

"This is Chelsea Snow."

*I*t was the end. Mary was not the first one to see it scroll up, like at the end of a movie, but she was not the last, either. It was 1976. Carter had just been elected. Snowbird was going to day care at Friendship. Mary had started taking horticulture classes at a community college. Larry had finished his alternative duty sentence and was now working for a farmer down the road. For over two years he had been gone every night, sleeping days. Now he was gone even more.

It was just the three of them by then, and Mary was lonely. Curt and Shelley left for McCall, Idaho, in 1973, and then headed back to Kansas a few years later when Curt got a job teaching. Bob and Fern left early, too, moving into an old neighbor's house and taking care of her in exchange for room and board, then headed southeast in a truck with a camper-back that Bob spent *a year building a foot too wide to be legal. Cunningham fell in love with a woman named Linda and moved with her and her two boys to Cottage Grove outside Eugene. Randy Aldrich followed a few years later. Elliott, who left and then came back, left for the final time with Krista, and also moved to Eugene. And Donnie moved into Iowa City to better manage the properties his aunts owned.*

So Mary spent the winter days alone, baking bread, listening to music and staring out the window. It was hard. When Larry had the car she was stuck on the farm. In the winter almost no one stopped by and you can only do so much yoga in a day. Meanwhile, out in the world the women's movement was in full swing, and Mary was ready to prove herself. She wanted to join Gloria Steinem's "Post Patriarchal Society" and get to deconstructing. Besides, she was not so sure the world was such a bad place anymore. The war was over. She was ready to give living in civilization a second chance. But Larry didn't understand. He was fine. He was fine on the farm, fine having things be just the way they had always been.

So she decided to leave.

What follows is not the confrontation I wanted—not the weeping and begging and screaming of two people dissecting a life together—but the matter of factness of the long overdue.

It is Mary standing in the kitchen, her long hair cut shoulder length, her hands on her hips. It is Larry standing too far away from her, his hair and beard longer than they have ever been. It is Mary saying, I am leaving. I am going into to town to be closer to school. I am renting one of Donnie's apartments. I am not coming back.

It is Larry saying, I don't understand. I don't understand. I don't understand.

It is Mary and Snowbird packing their boxes and moving into the blue house in Iowa City.

Larry stayed at the farm for months after that, all alone. It was the dead of winter, when even the woodstove could not keep the house from freezing at night and there was nothing to do but listen to the new Bob Dylan album over and over again. He was in sad shape when an old college friend finally drove out for a visit. You can't stay here, the friend told him. You have to go on with your life. The friend told Larry about a job counseling troubled kids. Larry applied, and got the position. It is a field he will be in the rest of his professional life. But there was too much snow and mud to commute every day from the country. And so Larry, the last idealist, moved into town.

The day he drove away for the final time there was a heavy snow. He had given away or sold all the animals except Sorrel, and the house was empty and cold. He saved a couple of things: the albums, some clothes, his banjo. He couldn't help feeling as if something had been left behind, though, so not far down the road he pulled over alongside the ditch to glance back for one last look, but the old farmhouse had already disappeared into a whirl of white.

What to do if you get lost.
Before you start out, whether it is
immediately after the waiting
period, or the next morning,
write a note if possible (pencil
and paper, charcoal on bark) and
fasten it with pegs to your marked
tree. Give your name, which
way you went, and the date.
—The Handbook for Boys,
Boy Scouts of America

My mother's friend Frank tells the story of how he used to go to Martha's Vineyard when he was young. There was a stretch of private property that he especially liked, and since the owners were rarely there he would spend hours sitting on the shore, watching the water. It was his special place, his sanctuary, and he would go there whenever he was depressed, taking a rock from the beach when he would leave. Long after he had stopped going to that beach he still had the collection of rocks.

One day, an acquaintance was visiting Frank in Iowa and she commented on how she had a similar collection. Frank told the woman where he had picked his up, and the woman paled.

Of course, it turned out it had been her property Frank had been trespassing on.

I'm not sure what it is that I like most about this story. I like the surprise, the unexpected revelation. But I also like the idea that there are people out there with your same collection of rocks.

I like to think that the farm was a little bit like that, that for those of us who lived there, it was a place and time that will be with us always. Donnie has told me that it saved his life, that if he had stayed with Cora any longer he would be crazy or dead by now. Teresa, I think, is still trying to get back. As for my parents, they talk about those years the way my grandfather used to talk about his years as a bombardier in World War II, as if somehow the air was clearer and you could breathe in more of it.

Since I've come back a lot of people have asked me why on earth I decided to return to Iowa after all these years.

I tell them that I've come back to pick up rocks.

I am sitting on the bed remembering all this when Snowbird comes in. Her wild, blonde hair is wilder than usual and her red dress is dirty. She sees me and stands in the doorway on the sides of her feet, the way that I still do sometimes, her hands in tight fists. She looks at me with her hard little blue eyes. Squints. Raises an eyebrow. Waits.

"It's me," I tell her. "I've come back to help you look for berries."

Epilogue

ugust 1995. I have been in Iowa a year when my mother surprises us all and returns to the States after six months in Mexico. "I can live in America," she explains. "Now that I know I can live someplace else."

We have both looked for, and found something, my mother and I. She has found herself again, sipping mescal with the Mayan women at a cafe in San Cristobal. In the process she has recovered the unrecoverable. She has recovered her spirit.

Never quite as dramatic as my mother, my recognition is a process. I live in my skin here. I wake up in the morning and I am amazed at the very fact that I am back. I have recovered something, but it is not my parents or the farm—I have always had those. It is more a recognition of my relationship to them.

I live in Iowa. Where I lived on a farm with my whacked-out hippie pothead parents. I called my parents by their first names until I was nine and strung my own love beads. My name used to be Chelsea Elizabeth, but now it's Chelsea Snow again, and my hippie name was Snowbird. My mother is the Snowqueen. I weave a mean God's Eye. My father was tear-gassed three times. And if you want to know what my parents have given me, ask me sometime what I think about the Republican-controlled Congress.

That's the politics of it; the personal is this: She is my wild abandon. My indestructible drop. My Original Nature. I was as far away from her in Irvine, California, as I have ever been in my life.

The first month my mother was in Mexico, I flew down from Iowa and met her in the Yucatan. We traveled to Merida, the capital of the province and one of the oldest cities in the country, and then to Cancun.

There are two buses you can take to get from Merida to Cancun. The first, and most inexpensive, is the second-class bus. This is the one the locals take. It stops often, has no air conditioning and the wind tunnel effect resulting from the open windows will leave you picking bugs out of your teeth for weeks. On the bright side, the bus drivers are allowed to decorate as they please (picture Maria de Guadalupe framed with clusters of plastic poinsettias and flickering lights) and the blasting radio will keep you abreast of the latest Mexican trends in music.

Your other choice is the premiere "europea" class. For twice the pesos, you can arrive in half the time. This is the bus the tourists take because they like the thick blue curtains that cover the windows and the American films on the television monitors and the seats that recline when you press the button on the armrest. On this bus you will be able to meet people who you went to college with or who are related to someone you went to college with or who have dated someone who applied to where you went to college but didn't get in.

I know this, because my mother and I barreled down the Yucatan peninsula in bus number two at speeds I can only estimate to be well over 200 miles per hour.

How my mother and I came to be there, in the center of the Yucatan, in the midst of an historic economic crisis and tension of insurrection, is the result of a last minute fervor of spontaneity that in other people might have resulted in buying a two pound bag of M & M's, but in my mother and me is much more dangerous.

Our Mayan guide: "What brought you here?"

My mother (after deep consideration): "Destiny."

Our Mayan guide: "No. I mean did you take a bus?"

We spent eleven days in Merida. Every day we were there a pro-Zapatista demonstration was held in the main plaza down the street from our hotel. Every day we saw more men with guns. Every day the peso dropped another dollar. And every day my mother became more and more convinced that this was where she had to be.

Our Mayan guide told us that if you go into the jungle expecting to see snakes then you will see many, but if you go in expecting to see none you can walk across the entire jungle without seeing any. I told him that we had that in the U.S. too, only we called it "denial." But my mother saw his story differently. "It's about choosing how to live," she said.

Later, sitting on that bus watching Sean Connery and Lorraine Bracco fall in love and listening to the Americans behind me discuss how slow Mexicans are and how they litter too much, I found myself pulling back the blue cloth secured with snaps over the window next to my seat and pressing my forehead against the glass to catch a glimpse of the blurred outside world. Next time, my mother and I told each other that day, we were going to take the second-class bus—the one without curtains.

My childhood bus was that slow one, the one you could see out of. But the older and further away I got, the faster it became.

A lot of people lose touch with their childhoods. But there was so much invested in mine. I was the only kid on the farm. It was the early seventies, and the hippie movement had already been proclaimed dead. The Manson Family had killed Sharon Tate and her unborn baby. The president had resigned in disgrace. Even the Beatles had broken up. From the porch of that old farmhouse in Iowa, it must have looked as if the country were falling apart. "It was a time in which everything seemed possible," my mother told me once, "which was wonderful, until we realized that those possibilities included Patty Hearst with an Uzi."

So they turned inward, and as their reality seemed to be dying, they tried to give as much of it to me as they could. "All of us have become a family," my mother wrote to a friend the day I was born, "and now we have a new baby." Of course, they have all moved on now. They have all moved on, and I am here.

I suppose there was no escaping it. Even Richard Nixon would return home when times got tough. He knew he looked ridiculous pacing the beaches of San Clemente in his suit and loafers. But he just couldn't help it. There was simply something about that salt air that reminded him of his first date with Pat, or the day Tricia was born, or long walks with Checkers, or maybe what it was like to just sit, before everything had all gone to hell. If his ghost haunts us now, it is on that beach, as a part of Snowbird will always haunt that farmhouse.

After my mother returns from Mexico, she visits me in Iowa City. It is important, she explains, for her to reconnect with the place one more time, as I have. We see Donnie and Frank and Teresa and drive the old country roads. I have been in Iowa long enough to be able to really show her my places, as she showed me hers only a year before. She loves seeing me here, in this place of her past. It's like remembering a dream, she says.

When she gets back to Portland she buys a new car—a red Subaru station wagon with a ski rack on the roof. But before she can drive it much, she comes down with a nasty flu. A week later, she goes to see her doctor. At first they think she has contracted malaria in Mexico, but the truth is revealed with an ultrasound. The cancer has returned. More tests follow: CAT scans, MRIs. There are tumors in her bile duct, her lungs, her brain. The melanoma has metastasized as we somehow always knew it would.

We've told the doctors we don't want to know statistics, but their grim expressions tell it all. They say there is nothing to do but wait, as if waiting is an action in itself. But my mother is a Buddhist, and understands the art of mindfulness. She is like the monk falling from a tall building. "So far, so good," he cries halfway down.

When I first join her in Portland, she tells me not to worry. She tells me that after the first diagnosis, she felt overwhelming regret for the things she hadn't done. This time, she says, she doesn't feel that way. She has lived how she has wanted to. She has been herself. She has been true to her own wonderful, Snowqueen bodhisattva wisdom.

Since my mother's diagnosis, I have had eight biopsies, two of which have been borderline melanomas. As long as they excise them in time, I am not in danger, but sometimes when I am sitting alone at night I watch the skin on my arm and shoulder and I think I can see the cells quietly mutating. I trace the moles with my fingers, memorizing their shape so I will know if they grow bigger. I watch new freckles for signs of atypia and worry about unexplained pains in my stomach or chest.

I am not going to die of cancer, but sometimes I have to remind myself of this. So I think about what is important. About how I want to be. About those summer nights on the farm and my mother and how the Snowqueen always said she would watch over me. And I think about living.

I have this memory, from when I was about thirteen, of driving out into the country with my mother to watch the harvest moon rise. We drove for about an hour on these dark country roads with numbers instead of names. It was past midnight and a school night and I remember that I was very tired—all I wanted was to turn back. I begged to go home, whining about how early I had to get up and how bored I was. But my mother kept driving. And then, suddenly, she pointed off toward the horizon. Rising above a dark field, as if she conjured it, was this huge moon—a great, orange heavenly body. It was the most beautiful thing I had ever seen. There we were, my mother and me, out in the middle of nowhere, watching this natural phenomenon, and there were no other people out there. There were no other cars, no farms—just us. Because we had gone looking for it. Because we had driven into the dark, trusting in the experience. Because she kept driving.

Self-knowledge is a funny thing—it is, I've decided, less discovery than acceptance. For me, it is in the recognition of where I come from. It is my parents' stubborn pride in having supported McGovern and in the fading photographs of their pasts. It is the smell of marijuana after dinner, it is an old antiwar poster, it is a "Pegasus for President" campaign button. And it is in the stories I grew up on.

So I walk. And I remember. As I tap my umbrella against the pavement, I feel I am moving forward. I am learning. Do I know anything more about the universe than when I started out? No. But I know Donnie and I know Frank. I know which road to take out of Iowa City to get to the three farms we lived on. I know how tall the tree is my mother and I planted in front of that brown house when I was six. And I know this:

I am still a product of this place. And as I go out into the big world to hunt for berries, it is with my parents' joy, cynicism, rage, revelry, hope, honesty, conviction and devastation. It is with Donnie, Elliott, Cunningham, Shelley, Curt and the Snowqueen. It is with that porch light and riding down Duval Street with my dad and the Grateful Dead playing through kitchen speakers. It is with banjo music and magic moon dust and eating tomatoes right off the vine. And it is with the knowledge that somehow I am still that blonde, little girl running naked through the vegetable garden.

I am still Snowbird.

About the Author

Chelsea Snow Cain spent her early childhood on a commune in Iowa before moving to Washington State with her mother. She graduated from University of California, Irvine, and received a master's degree in journalism from the University of Iowa. She lives in Portland, Oregon, where she works as a freelance writer. *Dharma Girl* is her first book. She is currently working on a second book, this time—"to my parents' relief"—fiction.